Contents

GW00787844

Preface   vi

Foreword to First Edition   viii

Preface to First Edition   ix

1 Sea Law: an Introduction   1
Caution – naming a ship – ship's library – sea lawyers – sea law
– whom to consult – definitions: yacht, vessel, ship, small ship,
hovercraft, boat, craft, launch, houseboat, harbour, waters,
wreck (jetsam, flotsam, lagan) – reading list

2 Acquiring a Craft   13
Cost – contract – advertisements – deposits – subject to contract
– buying new – Lloyds' yacht services – penalty clauses –
insolvency of builder – buying secondhand – brokers – marina
sales – commission – particulars – private sales – bill of sale –
deliveries – auctions – surveyors – Unfair Contract Terms Act –
marine mortgage – hire-purchase – bank loan – sharing –
charter: procedure, security deposit, delay, charterparty –
registration – application – name – declaration of ownership –
survey – carving – certificate of registry – small ships' register –
flags – special ensigns

3 Insurance   47
Marine insurance – insurable interest – proposal form – duty of
disclosure – valuation – personal effects – total and partial loss –
limitation of liability – third party risks – standard yacht policy
– in commission/laid up – use – loss/damage – repairs – no
claims – medical – legal – trailers – safety requirements – gas
installations – fuel – fire extinguishers – life jackets and safety
harness – flares – radar – outboards – tenders – racing risks –

salvage charges – marinas – dinghies – windsurfers – illegality –
arbitration – renewal date – transfer – complaints – cancellation
– check your cover

4   Ashore, Afloat and Aground   65
Moorings – marinas – safety rules – salvage – liens – tow –
lifeboats – rescue services – no cure: no pay-cost of salvage –
HM Coastguard – harbour master – marking wrecks – pilotage
and light dues – repairs

5   Rules of the Road   78
Collision rules – statutory rules – court rulings – Maritime
Conventions Act 1911 – sailing and steering rules: look out and
safe speed, giving way, narrow channels – traffic separation
schemes – lights – sailing vessels under way and vessels under
oars – anchored – River Thames – rule in the *Bywell Castle* –
recording collisions – reporting – log

6   Venturing Overseas   94
Documents – colours – insurance – notice of departure – foreign
arrival – return – quick report – full report – stores –
immigration – drugs – customs duties on yachts – importation –
rabies – duty free – quarantine – search – forfeiture – Customs
and Excise Management Act 1979 – arrest – Channel Islands –
France – trailers – Republic of Ireland – discipline

7   Civil Sea Law   109
Limited liability – racing – negligence – contributory negligence
– careless anchoring – careless berthing – careless diving –
dangerous wash – dangerous gash – fire precautions – volenti –
crew – privileged wills – charts – time limits – burden of proof –
civil proceedings – arbitration

8   Criminal Sea Law   121
The courts – foreign law – navigation – manslaughter –
dangerously unsafe ship – submarine cables – false signals –
buoys – Public Health Acts – foreshore – trespassers – banned
areas – oil rigs – joy riding – criminal damage – lobster pots –
oyster beds – crime prevention – arrest – nuisance – births and
deaths – blight by boats – firearms – fishery limits – radio –
duty to assist

Brian Calwell

Sea Lawyer

A Practical Guide for Yachtsmen

with cartoons by Bill Beavis

Second edition

ADLARD COLES LIMITED
8 Grafton Street, London W1

Adlard Coles Ltd
William Collins Sons & Co. Ltd
8 Grafton Street, London W1X 3LA

First edition published in Great Britain by
Granada Publishing in Adlard Coles Ltd 1980
Second edition published by
Adlard Coles Ltd 1986

Distributed in the United States of America
by Sheridan House, Inc.

Copyright © Brian Calwell 1980, 1985

British Library Cataloguing in Publication Data
Calwell, Brian
Sea lawyer: a practical guide for yachtsmen.—
2nd ed.
1. Yachts and yachting—Law and legislation—
England
I. Title
344.204'99   KD2755

ISBN 0-229-11762-7

Typeset in Great Britain by
V & M Graphics Ltd, Aylesbury, Bucks
Printed and bound in Great Britain by
Mackays of Chatham, Kent

To Marian, who has helped weather many a storm, and to the
memory of Ian, and all who sailed in *Heather*, RCC.

9   Boats on Wheels   141

Law on wheels – trailer law – on the road – trailer – insurance
and test certificate – learners and passengers – immobilising
detached trailer – secure loads – miscellaneous points: overall
length, overall width, total weight, invalid carriage, motor cycles,
springs, mirrors, wings, brakes, tyres, lights, marking, speed
limits, roadside checks – trailing in France – Belgium – in
general

Useful Addresses   150

Index   158

Preface

Mark Twain writing of his life on the Mississippi as a cub pilot tells how his mentor stopped singing 'Father in heaven the day is declining' and asked: 'What's the name of the first point above New Orleans?' Twain continues, 'I was grateful to answer promptly and I did. I said I did not know.' There must be many who find themselves in a similar position when presented with points of law of which, by what has been described as a fanciful fiction of our constitution, all are deemed to be aware.

This second revised edition seeks to spell out the answers, as painlessly as possible, to those who mess about in boats, and to help keep them on the windy side of the law.

The law, in common with the Goodwin Sands, is, in the words of the *Dover Strait Pilot*, an ever shifting and changing scene 'littered with wrecks'. This second edition charts changes in the rules as to registration, privileged ensigns, limitation of liability and the Collision Regulations. It has been extended to include extra material on such matters as chartering, CB radio, windsurfing, contributory negligence and useful addresses. Escalating marina and mooring charges have persuaded increasing numbers to join the fleet of sailor trailers on the roads and so a fresh chapter has been added to speed them on their way.

I am grateful to all who assisted in launching the first edition and repeat the acknowledgments I made in that preface. On this occasion I owe a special word of thanks to Mr Nicholas Evans, Honorary Secretary of the Bar Yacht Club, who has so cheerfully given me the benefit of his most experienced advice. I am also most appreciative of the ready aid given by officers of HM Coastguard and HM Customs and Excise, both at the

London Boat Show, where they excelled themselves, and elsewhere. I am further indebted to both the Automobile Association and to Mr David Suter of *Sally Ho* for providing information on trailing and chartering respectively. If I have got it wrong it is certainly not their fault.

I am obliged to the reviewers of the first edition, particularly to that learned contributor to the Law Society's *Guardian Gazette*, Mr Peter F. Carter-Ruck, who wrote: 'since this book will surely without doubt go into a second edition there are one or two points worth mentioning'. I have tried to include these and others to which my attention was so helpfully drawn and I am grateful to Mr Peter Coles, my publishers' Commissioning Editor, for his encouragement and for granting me a fair wind to update and expand this edition. Finally all tribute to Mr Charlie Chester of the BBC who appealed nationwide for the solution to an abstruse query which a reader had raised and which had momentarily eluded me.

Weather and sea conditions have, as the coastguards say, always a law to themselves and can never be wholly mastered. That too is true of the law of the realm. May this guide for lay persons to the topic, alleviated by the brilliant cartoons of Bill Beavis and tricked out, as the old lady said of *Hamlet*, by so many quotations, give aid if not comfort to those who go down to the sea on boards or in ships.

Brian Calwell
Middle Temple
21st October 1985

Foreword to the First Edition

It is a pity that to call a man a sea lawyer should be interpreted as a form of abuse, for some knowledge, however rudimentary, of the law of the sea should be part of the armoury of every mariner. For the yachtsman it is important to know at least something of how the law affects his boat, his crew, his dealings with his yard, his insurance company and his fellow-sailors. The appearance of this book is a timely reminder of what, for far too many yachtsmen, is a distinct gap in their knowledge, and Brian Calwell is to be congratulated for the judicious blend of erudition and lightness of touch which will make filling that gap a pleasurable exercise for all of us. To the many new-comers to the sport the passages on acquiring a craft and insuring it are really essential reading before taking any irrevocable step along the road to ownership, but even the most experienced owner or skipper will find within these pages food for thought and, more important, fresh enlightenment. As an indispensable work of reference this book should find its way into the library of every well-found yacht and I commend it to my fellow-yachtsmen in the expectation rather than the hope that it may help to prevent the avoidable legal contretemps and mitigate the unpleasantness of the unavoidable.

Sir Hugh Forbes
Royal Courts of Justice
London

Preface to the First Edition

My thanks are due to Mr Peter Rountree for suggesting the compilation of a layman's guide to basic yachting law and for his many constructive comments. I must also record my appreciation to Mr Gordon Fairley of the quite indispensable Royal Yachting Association, for letting me have a sight of various legal information sheets and pamphlets prepared over the last decade by himself and a number of RYA committee members, including Judge Andrew Phelan of both that body and the Bar Yacht Club. These have all been most useful in establishing the parameters of the practical topics which concern the average yachtsman.

Acknowledgments are also due to HMSO, to the Registrar General of Shipping and Seamen, to the Department of Trade, and in particular to their marine librarian at Sunley House.

The list of those who helped in dealing with queries both by correspondence, and over the telephone, is long, as witnessed by the addresses given in the appendix, but among those who should be mentioned are the RNLI, the Naval Division of the Ministry of Defence, HM Customs and Excise, the Director of Marine Operations of the Port of London, the Metropolitan Police, the Post Office External Communications Executive to the Maritime Radio Services Division, the Harbour Master at Cowes, Campbell Allan of the British Sub Aqua Club, my insurers Newton Crum, and of course Lloyd's.

None of the above is responsible in any way for any shortcomings there may be, for the views expressed are those of the author alone.

Finally I gladly record my gratitude to Mr Jeremy Howard Williams, aided and ably abetted as he was by Mr James

Skellorn, for constant encouragement, assistance and advice without which this venture would have vanished without trace at an early stage.

Brian Calwell
Middle Temple
21st October 1979

1　Sea Law

The law the lawyers know about,
Is property and land.
But why the leaves are on the trees,
And why the waves disturb the seas,
They do not understand.
H.P.D. Pepler
'The Law the Lawyers Know'

Caution

This guide to sea law starts with two cautions. The first echoes words often found in sailing directions and charts that, though all care has been taken, responsibility cannot be accepted for any mishap which may result from any unfortunate error. The second stresses that section 6 of the Interpretation Act 1978 applies throughout and thus the masculine gender includes females.

Naming a ship

Although statutes, collision regulations and harbour byelaws refer to ships as 'she', the owner of a yacht may call his craft by any name he pleases save that the name of a Part 1 registered British ship must be approved by the Registrar General of Shipping and Seamen. Consent will not be given if there is already a registered ship of that name, or if it so closely resembles that of another vessel as to deceive. Once named she shall not be described by any other.

Ship's library

All are deemed to know the law; ignorance is no excuse. Amateurs afloat are taken to be aware of the vast body of civil and criminal, and of national and international rules and regulations which combine to produce a maritime code. Accordingly the average yachtsman's library should at least include sailing directions, nautical almanacs, tidal atlases,

International Code of Signals, *Mariner's Handbook*, the International Regulations for Preventing Collisions at Sea, the *Seaway Code* and a copy of the local byelaws. The Merchant Shipping (Carriage of Nautical Publications) Rules 1975 apply to British registered ships of 12m and over in length which go to sea; it requires such vessels to carry proper charts and up to date information and publications. These and other regulations can be traced through the Department of Transport's Merchant Shipping Notice M 1154 *Principal Acts and Regulations* (HMSO) and in the annual list of *Merchant Shipping Notices* currently in force obtainable from the Marine Library (DOT).

Every well-found cruiser, as illustrated by Erskine Childers' *Dulcibella*, needs a good library. Slocum in his epic account of his circumnavigation tells of how with a stock of books on board he fell to reading day and night, leaving this pleasant occupation merely to trim sails while *Spray* nibbled at the miles. Conrad in his classic, *The Mirror of the Sea*, narrates that his favourite book was Stevens on *Stowage*: 'a portly volume with the renown and weight of Coke or Littleton which gives you the official teaching on the whole subject, is precise as to rules, mentions illustrative events, quotes case laws and is never pedantic.' Kurt Carlsen, who so heroically stayed with his stricken ship *Flying Enterprise* for 14 days in a Channel gale, found solace in reading and re-reading the only book in his cabin *The Seaman and the Law*. Donald Crowhurst, who set sail in 1969 in his trimaran *Teignmouth Electron* on a non-stop round-the-world race, became so unbalanced that he tragically attempted to win by deception. He supplemented his library as part of the plot by composing *A Song of the Southern Ocean* which included the lines:
'Unlike the muddled law of man,
Sea law is simple and true'.

Sea lawyers

The ordinary skipper probably thinks that, in turning a Nelsonic eye to the baffling literature of the law, he may with good luck and good insurers get by without disaster. His earnest wish will be to avoid any disputes over accounts from yards and chandlers; misguided manoeuvres resulting in collision and negotiations for a tow are matters which he feels he can play off the cuff should need arise. The fact is that a skipper has a duty to his ship, to all who sail in her, and to other users of the high seas and inland waters. He should at least read, mark and digest the terms of his insurance policy, as also certain key entries on his responsibilities in a nautical almanac. The prudent skipper should know his legal limitations and so assess when best to seek professional aid; such aid should be got from a qualified sea lawyer. The cunning of the shark has earned it the nickname of 'sea lawyer'. It makes a good natured appearance in the insignia of the Law Society Yacht Club, whose solicitorial members may be consulted with greater confidence than their fo'c'sle or barrack room counterparts.

Sea law

The law of England and Wales to which the yachtsman will normally turn comes from the common law, statute and the rules of equity as recorded in the law reports in which the Lloyd's series leads, but leaving, maybe, Sir Alan Herbert's celebrated *Misleading Cases* not so far behind. This law shares much with the law of Scotland, Northern Ireland, the Isle of Man and the Channel Islands, as also with the Commonwealth, but there are also big differences between these systems.

Common law goes back to the reign of Richard I and beyond. It helps when considering the rules of contract as to the buying and selling of a boat, or of tort when examining the duty to navigate with care. Statute law comprises parliamentary measures. From the reign of King John there is a continuous line of legislation of which one of the longest, the Merchant Shipping Act of 1894, is a conspicuous example. As Lord Kenyon commented in 1795, the legislature has anxiously provided for that most useful and deserving body of men, the seamen and mariners of this country. At the local level bye-laws made under delegated powers govern waterways. Thus the Port of London Authority may lay down rules as to the Thames, while bye-laws, typical of others, operate at Cowes. These control pleasure and commercial traffic, the hovercraft and chain ferry; they also restrict anchorage, and ban skiing, windsurfing and diving without the permission of the Harbour Master.

The rules of equity stem from the practices of the court of Chancery. They aid in tracing rights of way to the shore, and in resolving differences between partners. They set out the duty of candid disclosure when insuring.

Centuries ago, the seamen of England were bound by the Rhodian code of Oleron which declared that if a pilot through ignorance should cause a ship to miscarry, he should make full satisfaction or lose his head. The death penalty is not exacted now for such misadventures, but modern mariners voyaging east of Suez might bear in mind that there are certain ports where the ancient principle of an eye for an eye and a tooth for a tooth still holds sway. One sailor in such waters reported to the police that his camera had been stolen and identified the alleged culprit, whose hand was promptly chopped off. Later the complainant found the camera which had been mislaid and thought it only right to say so. The local court ordered that he too lose a hand.

The civil jurisdiction of the Queen's courts still runs (in the tongue of antiquity) to matters arising in inland tidal waters, and in the main streams of great rivers, and on the high seas, and to places where great ships go below the bridges where the tide ebbs and flows. Hence in a dispute between rival divers about their right to work on a wreck outside territorial waters, an English court granted an injunction; so too, compensation was awarded for damages caused by a ship to a jetty at Lagos. On the other side of the line, a Crown Court has said that its criminal jurisdiction did not extend to an abandoned anti-aircraft tower outside territorial waters, though it does now cover oil rigs.

A British ship is taken to be a floating island to which English law applies. In deciding whether the ship be British or not, a good test is to look to the nationality of the owner and to the flag the craft is wearing.

4

Whom to consult

The RYA evolved from the Yacht Racing Association, first founded in 1875 to regulate the organisation and administration of yacht racing in Britain; in 1953 it became the Royal Yachting Association. It is the national boating authority acting as Ombudsman, negotiator and organiser for all boat owners, and is affiliated to the International Yacht Racing Union. As the yachtsman's national authority, it is concerned with boats under sail or power, racing or cruising, inspecting upward of 500 sailing establishments and advising clubs. It monitors all proposed legislation and EEC regulations affecting yachtsmen, and it keeps a weather eye on harbours, planning and pleasure boat byelaws. The cruising department looks at Merchant Shipping Regulations as also buoyage, navigation and traffic separation. The RYA gives advice about marine mortgages, hire-purchase and yacht insurance. It issues certificates of identification and overseas helmsman's credentials. It liaises with harbour boards, fairway committees, Trinity House, marina operators, rating authorities and many other bodies. It publishes booklets dealing with registration, insurance, clubs, salvage etc., and in addition stocks over 150 information sheets on legal and other matters. It administers the Small Ships' Register on behalf of the Department of Transport; it is one of the organisations approved by the Department of Trade for the issue of a certificate to the Registrar as to the tonnage measurement of pleasure yachts under 45 feet (13.7m). It acts as an agent of the Ministry of Defence in connection with Admiralty permits as to the wearing of privileged Ensigns by yachts. Since 1983 the government has delegated to it the responsibility for examinations for VHF radio operator certificates.

Samuel Pepys would have greatly valued the services of the RYA, had it existed in his day, for it would have helped him to overcome the sense of ignorance which he confided to his diary: 'Lord what a shame methinks to me, in this condition and at this age, I should know no better the laws of my country.'

The aim of this book is to brief the yachtsman in lay terms as to the law of the sea, so that those who go down to the waters in

5

little ships may read as they run the index, at least, if not the text. Dr Johnson, who lived among lawyers, once said: 'Knowledge is of two kinds. We know a subject, or we know where we can find information upon it.' The fact that he also said; 'When men come to like a sea life they are not fit to live on land', need not detract from the wisdom of the earlier remark.

Definitions

Yacht

The term 'yacht' from the Dutch 'jacht' (to hunt) was introduced into England in 1660 by Charles II. A yacht is any vessel propelled by sails or by mechanical power, designed for pleasure purposes and not plying for hire. Pleasure yachts not exceeding 15 net registered tons which are only used on rivers, or the coasts of the United Kingdom where the owner resides, are exempt from compulsory registration and pilotage.

Vessel

'Vessel', from the French 'vaissel', includes any ship or boat, or any other description of vessel used in navigation. Under the Collision Regulations it covers every description of water craft, including non-displacement craft and seaplanes used as a means of transportation on water. A 'sailing vessel' means any vessel under sail, provided that propelling machinery if fitted is not being used.

Ship

A 'ship', an evolution from the old English word 'scip', under the 1894 Act includes every description of vessel or boat whatsoever used in navigation not propelled by oars. In former times 'ship' described a sailing vessel with a bowsprit and three masts. Now it is taken in popular parlance to be any large sea-going vessel propelled by sail or power. For Customs purposes there is a wider definition.

Small ship

The Merchant Shipping Act 1983 which introduced the Small

Ships' Register makes provision as to the measurement of small ships for length instead of tonnage. It defines such as a ship less than 24 m in length.

Hovercraft

All will admire and applaud the genius of the draftsman of the Hovercraft Act 1968 in which this newcomer to the nautical scene is defined as: 'a vessel which is designed to be supported in motion wholly or partly by air expelled from the vehicle to form a cushion of which the boundaries include the ground, water or other surface beneath the vehicle.' The Collision Regulations 1983 provided that an air cushion vessel when operating in the non-displacement mode shall exhibit in addition the the normal lights an all-round flashing yellow light. By section 81 of the Customs and Excise Management Act 1979 a hovercraft of whatever size is described as a small ship.

Boat

'Boat' is a term strictly speaking confined to a small open craft without any decking which is normally propelled by oars. A 'fishing boat' is any vessel for the time being employed in fishing operations.

Craft

A 'craft' is a boat or vessel of any kind. Under the 1894 Act, as amended, it is an offence for any craft (other than one propelled by oars) to carry more than 12 passengers (whether fare-paying or not) without a passenger certificate. It matters not that the passengers are actively engaged in rendering services aboard. Thus a conviction was imposed in the case of *The Bische* in 1983 where a gaff-rigged yawl took more than a dozen young persons on an excursion although they were actively helping to man the ship.

Pleasure craft arriving in, or departing from, the United Kingdom from or to places abroad are subject to the Pleasure Craft (Arrival & Report) Regulations 1979. A pleasure craft here means: (a) a vessel which, at the time of its arrival from abroad at a port in the UK, is being used for private recreational purposes and of which the total complement, including

7

passengers and crew, does not exceed 12 persons; or (b) any vessel which a Customs officer on written application agrees to treat as such.

Launch

A 'launch' under the Thames Water byelaws means any mechanically propelled vessel not being used solely as a tug or for the carriage of goods. 'Motor launch' is a launch propelled by an internal combustion engine.

Houseboat

In broad terms a 'houseboat' is any vessel used as a residence. The hull is generally insured on a marine policy as a cruising vessel in commission, even though its cruising range may be restricted to a few inches in any direction. The contents may be insured as house contents. So far, the courts have refused to accept that a houseboat is a dwelling within the meaning of the

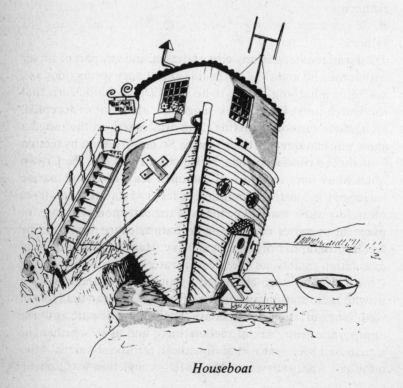

Houseboat

Rent Acts, and houseboat residents, although liable to pay rates, receive little or no protection against eviction from their moorings.

The British Waterways Act 1971 forbids the use of a houseboat on the Board's waterways without a valid certificate and mooring permit. A houseboat which is never used for cruising is not eligible for a permit to wear a privileged Ensign. A vessel is said to be used as a houseboat when she is not used under way, or navigating, but is used whilst on moorings or in her berth, by the owner or others for living on board.

Harbour

A harbour is a natural or artificial place where a ship may obtain shelter or services. The powers of a Harbour Master are derived from the Harbours, Docks and Piers Clauses Act 1857 and the Harbour Act 1964. 'Harbour Master' includes a dock master and any person specifically appointed by a harbour authority.

Waters

Tidal waters extend to any part of the sea, and any part of a river within the ebb and flow of the tide at ordinary spring tides and not being a harbour. It was in his book *De Domino Maris* that the Dutch jurist Bynershoek suggested, and nations accepted, his famous cannon shot rule. This was based on the range a shore gun could reach, then 3 miles. So now it is that, by section 7 of the Territorial Waters Jurisdiction Act 1878, the Crown holds sway over any part of the open sea within one marine league of the coast, i.e. 3 nautical miles (3.45 statute miles) from mean low water mark. The limits of the patrimonial sea are for practical purposes denoted on Admiralty charts produced by the Hydrographer of the Royal Navy. Hence a cartographical calculation establishes the area of waters which belong to the Crown. Charts were consulted by the court in the case of a private radio station transmitting from the old war-time fort of Red Sands off the Kentish coast. There was a dispute as to the appropriate base lines of measurement and as to whether the signals had been sent within or without territorial waters. After a look at Admiralty chart No. 1610 a conviction was upheld.

By the Fishery Limits Act 1976 territorial tidal waters extend to 200 miles from the sea baselines of the UK. The Continental Shelf Act 1964 gives effect to the Geneva Convention on the High Seas and provides for the exploration and exploitation outside territorial waters of the sea bed and subsoil and their natural resources; separate measures deal with oil rigs and pollution in navigable waters.

Wreck

'Wreck' is property cast ashore within the ebb and flow of the tide after shipwreck. It includes jetsam, flotsam, lagan and derelict found in or on the shores of the sea or any tidal water. *Jetsam* (jetzon) arises when a ship is in danger of being sunk and so as to lighten the vessel goods are jettisoned, or cast into the sea in an effort to save the ship and cargo.

Flotsam (flotzen) describes the wreck of a ship or of its cargo which is found floating.

Lagan (ligan) refers to goods cast from a foundering vessel into the sea which, owing to their weight, are specially buoyed or corked so as to aid their subsequent recovery.

Derelict is property, whether vessel or cargo, which has not sunk, but which has been abandoned at sea without hope of return or recovery.

Jetsam, flotsam or lagan picked up on the high seas belongs to the first finder, in default of an identified owner being traced. But when washed ashore, unclaimed wreckage belongs at common law to the Crown, and by statute is vested in the Receiver of Wreck unless the right has been granted to another. The finder of a wreck must notify the Receiver. In the case of unclaimed wrecks the Receiver is authorised where the goods are of low value, or so damaged, or of such perishable nature that they cannot be advantageously kept, to sell them forthwith or otherwise dispose of them within a year. An owner of a wreck in the possession of the Receiver, upon establishing his claim within a year may, upon payment of the salvage fees and expenses due, possess the wreck or its proceeds.

Reading list

This book cannot hope to do justice to all the reader's problems; the only safe advice if in legal doubt is to see a solicitor. If all that is needed is a wider view of the law, here is a suggested reading list:

General
The Law of the Sea William McFee (Faber)
The Law for Small Boats Andrew Phelan (Charles Knight)
You and the Law RYA Gen 10/84
Consumer Protection for Boat Users A.A. Painter (Nautical)
Surveying Small Craft Ian Nicolson (Adlard Coles Ltd)
Buying or Selling a Boat Colin Jarman (Adlard Coles Ltd)
Lloyd's Register Yacht & Small Craft Services
Reed's Nautical Almanac (Thomas Reed Publications Ltd)
Macmillan & Silk Cut Yachtsman's Handbook (Macmillan)

Special
The Collision Regulations RHB Sturt (Lloyd's of London Press Ltd)
Practical Pilotage Jeremy Howard-Williams (Adlard Coles Ltd)
Pleasure Craft Users' Guide to the Tidal Thames (PLA)
Thames River Users' Code (Thames Water)
The Charter Game Ross Norgrove (Nautical)
Trail & Sail Jacey Winters (Nautical)
Maritime Radio Services for Yachts (BTI Maritime) RYA publications
Solent Year Book (IOW County Press)

Reference
Halsbury's Laws of England (Butterworths)
British Shipping Laws (Stevens & Sons)
Archbold Criminal Pleading, Evidence and Practice (Sweet & Maxwell)
Every Man's Own Lawyer (Every Man's Own Lawyer Publishing)
Lloyd's Law Reports

Current Law Year Books (Sweet & Maxwell)
Channel Pilots Hydrographer to the Navy (HMSO)

Aids
Principal Regulations and Acts on Merchant Shipping (HMSO)
Current Merchant Shipping Notices (Department of Trade Marine Library)
Small Craft. Edition of Admiralty Notices to Mariners (MOD)
Mariners' Handbook (Hydrographic Department, MOD)
Water Sports Code (Sports Council)
Boating on the Waterways (British Waterways Board)
Seaway Code. A guide for small boat users (HMSO)

2 Acquiring a Craft

The crew was complete; it included a Boots –
A maker of Bonnets and Hoods –
A Barrister brought to arrange their disputes –
And a Broker to value their goods.

> *Lewis Carroll*
> 'The Hunting of the Snark'

Cost

The first consideration in acquiring a craft must be a financial
one. Is the cash to be raised by way of loan or a marine
mortgage, or perhaps from a partnership venture? For a few the
demand will be for a custom built boat, while at the other end of
the scale the enthusiast may be content with a DIY kit. But most
will turn to the new or secondhand market. The average buyer
will scan the classified advertisements appearing in the sailing
and national press, not overlooking the local papers and
Exchange & Mart. If he is cautious (for buying a boat is a
complex affair), he may limit his search to approved agents
recognised by the Yacht Brokers, Designers and Surveyors
Association or by the Association of British Yacht Agents.
Whatever his mode of acquisition, the ordinary rules of
contract obtain.

Contract

A contract is an agreement made between two or more parties
for value which is intended to be enforceable at law. It may be
made orally, or it may be made in writing. The transfer of a
registered British ship, which is required to be so registered, or
of any share therein, must be by a Bill of Sale. A contract of sale
is defined by the Sale of Goods Act 1979 as a contract whereby
the seller transfers, or agrees to transfer, the property in goods
to a buyer for a money consideration called the price. Before a
contract arises, there must be an offer on the one side and an
acceptance on the other side of the precise terms of that very

proposal. Such an offer must be distinguished from an *intention to make* an offer, and from an invitation to treat. An advertisement is an invitation to treat, and any apparent acceptance of its terms only gives rise to an offer, which the advertiser is free to accept or to reject. Thus if a yacht auction is advertised to be held at a certain time and place, and an expectant bidder travels at some expense on that date only to find that it has been cancelled, he is without legal redress. At an auction sale a request for bids is but a mere invitation to bargain, and acceptance of the highest bid only occurs on the fall of the hammer.

Advertisements

Normally editors, before accepting an advertisement, ask the client to warrant that the advertisement does not contravene any of the provisions of the Trade Descriptions Act 1968, and does not contain any defamatory or untrue statement, or infringe any copyright, patent or design; an offender may be liable to both criminal and civil penalty. The 1968 Act does not apply to private sellers. Nevertheless, all advertisers whether traders or otherwise may be civilly liable for false statements of facts. The law takes a more relaxed view of expressions of opinion which even if exaggerated may be accepted as legitimate trade puffs. Editors cannot guarantee the accuracy of all their trade entries, or indeed the solvency of their advertisers, and a buyer should make his own inquiries. Cases happen of advertisements appearing for the products of companies already in liquidation; this can lead to a loss of sums paid, and those who have parted with their money may find themselves in the hapless position of unsecured creditors.

The normal response to an advertisement for a new or secondhand boat is a request for further information; then negotiations as to price, time and delivery and other details take place between the parties. An actual enforceable agreement results only when everything which needs to be agreed has been settled and there is a state of *consensus ad idem* i.e. both parties are in harmony. Once a formal offer is accepted without reservation a valid agreement comes into existence. If there are

14

any reservations as to acceptance then these constitute a counter-offer. Once made an offer remains an offer until it is accepted, rejected, revoked or has lapsed.

A distinction must be made between advertisements and particulars of sale which, on request to boat builders or brokers, may be supplied either orally or in writing. These may on the face of the transaction amount to offers in themselves, to which the prospective buyer may reply by communicating his acceptance without further ado. Once accepted the contract is complete.

Deposits

The would-be purchaser under the terms of an agreement may be required to pay a sum of money in advance such as 10% of the price. It is a question of construction of the terms of the contract as to whether this amounts to part payment or a deposit. If clearly expressed to be by way of a deposit, its primary purpose is to indicate that the buyer means business. It is given as security and an earnest of good intention. It is recoverable if the deal goes off. If it goes on it is set off against the purchase price.

Subject to contract

A prospective buyer should safeguard himself against any legal pitfalls which may lead to his prematurely becoming owner of a boat. This he should do by heading all preliminary correspondence as 'subject to contract', or 'subject to survey'. The effect of these or of other such conditional words such as 'subject to marine mortgage', or to a valuation is to make it clear that all is still in a state of negotiation, and to ensure that he is not inadvertently introduced into a binding agreement until the embargo of those strictures is lifted.

Buying new

In buying a new production boat the first approach will be to the builders. This will produce particulars, often a brochure, describing the yacht, accompanied by a printed standard contract to be signed. It is desirable that this should be in the form approved by the Ship and Boat Builders National Federation. These documents repay detailed study and interpretation against the background of the law, and particularly the Sale of Goods Act 1979 and of the Supply of Goods (Implied Terms) Act 1973 which now limits the ability of sellers to exclude certain protective conditions and warranties. The brochure sets out in attractive form the price and specifications of the boat and also a list of optional equipment. Terms may vary from firm to firm. It is not unusual for a down payment of £200 to be made subject to contract, followed by some proportion such as 50 or $33\frac{1}{3}\%$ to be paid on signature of the confirmation order, perhaps with further instalments on progress of the work, and the balance 10 days before delivery. If he can, a buyer may wish to try and negotiate a money retention clause, as is standard in property building agreements, of 5% of the contract sum to allow for proper inspection and approval after delivery prior to final payment.

A contractual document may make it clear that delivery will only take place after full payment has been made, as against prices ruling at the date of the final invoice in accordance with the terms of business. The specification may be stated to be subject to variation without notification; all prices are subject to VAT; delivery charges, including carriage and insurance, may be the subject of a separate quotation.

In the case of a custom built boat the builders undertake to construct a craft as specified by the purchaser for an agreed price. Terms of payment may be: 10% with order; 15% when hull and deck moulded; 25% on installation of engine; balance 7 days prior to delivery. The contract may go on to narrate that all modifications are to be in writing; the craft to be delivered at a fixed date at a specified charge; there may be a minimum charge for delivery and rigging. In the event of completion being delayed by any cause beyond the builder's reasonable control, or by *force majeure*, then the delivery date shall be reasonably deferred. Charges may have to be adjusted should sub-contractors raise costs. The builders shall be deemed to have completed the construction of the craft in accordance with the requirements of the agreed specifications, on the signature of the Lloyd's Series Production certificate by the Society's surveyor. The builders undertake to insure the craft against all risks in accordance with the Institutes Clauses for Builders' Risks, as amended for yachts and motor boats. Under a defects liability clause, the builders may agree to make good by repair or compensation any defect in workmanship discovered in the hull, machinery or equipment of the craft within 6 months after delivery, fair wear and tear excepted. In the event of any instalment being unpaid 28 days after notice has been given, the builders will be at liberty to sell the boat and to turn to the customer for any loss they may sustain. An arbitration clause is commonly included.

Lloyd's Yacht Services

Those wishing to have their yachts built to the highest standards and from the best materials available would be well advised to enlist the aid of Lloyd's Register of Yacht and Small Craft Services in such matters as pre-contractual and post-delivery transactions; construction survey for certification and classification; classification of the yacht under the Society's survey in conformity with the relevant rules and, on completion, the assignment of a record of class, viz ✠ 100 A ✠R is assigned to racing yachts of the international classification. Lloyd's caution buyers to be careful and not to be misled by such terms as 'built to Lloyd's specifications' of which there is no such thing, or 'exceeds Lloyd's requirements' which is meaningless. The claim 'she's a Lloyd's boat' is easy to check either on sight of the certificate or by contacting the Society.

Penalty clauses

In order to encourage timely performance of a yacht building contract, it is not unusual to embody a clause which provides that, in the event of non-completion by an agreed date a sum of money at a fixed scale shall be paid for every week whereby the builder is in default. Whether such an amount is recoverable depends upon whether the court is satisfied that the figure reflects a realistic pre-estimate of the damage likely to be suffered. If the court is of the view that it is an extravagant amount and of a penal and extortionate nature, having no relation to the actual loss sustained, then it is irrecoverable. The test is that if the intention is to secure performance of the contract by the imposition of a fine then the sum specified is a penalty, but if on the other hand the intention is to assess genuinely the damages for breach of contract it is a liquidated amount and in order.

Insolvency of builder

The would-be buyer of a custom built or production craft should incorporate into the contract appropriate machinery to protect himself in the event of the builder becoming insolvent. Insolvency is an inability to pay debts as and when they fall due. A statutory declaration of insolvency can lead to bankruptcy in the case of an individual and to winding up in that of a limited company. On an adjudication of bankruptcy the property of the bankrupt is vested in a trustee and becomes divisible among his creditors. A customer may now find himself in some difficulties, for the trustee is entitled to claim all property within the reputed ownership of the bankrupt for the benefit of the body of creditors, and this may include boats on which advance payments have already been made. A buyer may seek to defeat the presumption that the boat was so claimable by insisting upon an advance term that the boat as she is constructed, and all materials from time to time intended for her whether in the builder's yard, workshop or elsewhere, shall immediately as the vessel takes shape become the property of the purchaser and shall not be within the ownership, control or disposition of the builders. It is a matter of contract in each case as to at what stage the property in a boat and its machinery is taken to pass from the builder to a customer, and an issue of fact in each case as to whether that stage has been reached. Risks may arise when machinery and navigational equipment is delivered to the builder's yard and invoiced to the builder though paid for by the customer. In an era of increasing insolvencies, a buyer would do well to enlist professional assistance before finalising the instalment stages of a boat-building agreement.

There is a clear need when entering into a boat building contract to look carefully at the insurance aspect and to be satisfied that there is appropriate cover for such contingencies as fire or theft after the property is deemed to pass to the buyer, and also to secure indemnity against loss in circumstances where the transfer of the boat to the purchaser is frustrated in the event of an adjudication of bankruptcy of a builder, or of liquidation, where the vendor is a limited company. A buyer may derive some measure of protection by making his agreement along the lines of the SBNF's standard form for the construction of new craft. If the transaction is being conducted through an agent a parallel contract with the builders should be considered.

In some cases it might be prudent to take a bank reference on the builder or to insist on a guarantee from his bank. Alternatively insurance against the possibility of the builder's insolvency, etc. may well be worth the premium.

Buying secondhand

In buying secondhand, if this is not done privately, an approach will normally be made to a broker. This may be by post or in person, and will usually lead to the buyer receiving particulars of various craft on offer. An experienced broker will ask a seller to sign a declaration that the vessel offered for sale is not the subject of any mortgage, hire-purchase agreement or any maritime, statutory or other lien, and is free from all incumbrances and restrictions. The seller may be invited to certify that the details of the craft are correct, and to undertake to indemnify the broker against claims of misrepresentation, as also accepting liability for all risks arising in the course of demonstration.

The owner may be further asked to declare: 'I wish you to place the craft on your Register at an asking price of £x (including brokerage commission), and I agree that should I place the craft with any other broker, or sales outlet, the asking price will coincide with the above. Should I wish to amend this figure I will advise you in writing.'

Brokers

The broker is an agent for the seller of the boat who is paid a commission on the sale. A seller may place his boat in the hands of a number of brokers, or he may instruct but one. In the latter event he may appoint such person as a 'sole agent' for the sale of the boat in which event, although free to sell himself, if it is sold through other brokers then double commission may have to be paid. If the broker is appointed as 'sole selling agent' this may allow him to recover commission even if the owner sells privately.

A point to watch is that a clause may be written into the agency agreement that, in the event of a private sale of the boat whilst on the broker's register, a sum of $1\frac{1}{2}\%$ of the gross sale price will be paid. Thus if the boat is in the hands of a number of brokers a private sale could prove expensive, especially if the boat is berthed at a marina under terms which require a vendor selling privately to pay one sixth of the standard brokerage commission to the marina.

Marina sales

A skipper who berths his boat at a marina when contemplating a sale should consult the conditions of mooring which he has accepted. A term may say that no sale shall take place within the marina without the written consent of the operators and that they shall be entitled to the payment of an access charge at the rate of 1% of the total sale price. Such a clause may perhaps be defeated if an owner so arranges the sale that the acceptance of his offer takes place otherwise than on the marina premises. A more tightly drafted rule may, however, make it more difficult for a berth holder to challenge the charge particularly if this has been approved by the Director General of Fair Trading. As far as he is able, an owner should seek at the outset when negotiating a berth or mooring at a marina or yacht harbour to have any restrictive conditions modified to allow of a genuine private sale without penalty.

Commission

As to the broker's commission one must look first to the contract. A good guide as to what is a reasonable scale is to be found in the Code of Practice set out by the British Boating Industry. The ordinary understanding of the courts is that commission is not payable on the introduction of a person who is willing and ready to buy the boat, but only on a completed sale. Introducing a purchaser willing to buy 'subject to satisfactory survey' is not good enough. Commission comes out of the purchase price paid, and the sale must be completed successfully before the fee is earned. Even if it goes off through the failure of the seller, the broker has no right of recovery for any expenses, unless these are the subject of specific agreement.

What happens if the owner meets a buyer through an agent and rejects his offer, but later agrees to sell behind the agent's back? The agent will of course be justified in claiming his commission, but at the same time each transaction must turn on its own facts, for it is not sufficient for the agent to show that the arrangement would not have been entered into but for his introduction. He must show that the introduction is the direct cause of the sale and that this really and substantially resulted from his acts.

Commission rates are normally agreed to be at the scale recommended by the Yacht Brokers, Designers and Surveyors Association, the Ship and Boat Builders National Federation, or by the Association of British Yacht Agents. A letter of acceptance by an agency may read: 'If we are successful in introducing a client who subsequently purchases the boat our commission will be calculated at 8% on the first £5000 and 6% on the residue plus VAT. Although priced at £10 000 any offers will naturally be submitted to you. If you have any further information regarding the price or location of the craft, or of course should you sell her yourself, perhaps you will be so good as to let us know. In the meantime we will use our best endeavours to sell your craft as soon as possible'. From this it will be seen that VAT is paid on a secondhand boat on the broker's commission, not on the value of the boat. If the boat is sold privately without the services of a broker, no VAT attaches.

Particulars

A broker now produces particulars of the boat. These may run: 1976, 26 foot auxiliary Bermudan sloop lying at Poole, price £9950'. Thereafter follow specifications, designer and builder, construction, sails, engine, tender, accommodation, water and fuel capacity, equipment. There may be added: 'this boat offers seakindly and comfortable cruising', and that a full inventory and a copy of a recent survey report are available for inspection. The broker may go on to point out that he is in a position to advise as to marine mortgage, insurance and registration, and in exceptional cases moorings.

On receipt of the particulars the buyer should note that the transaction is governed by the maxim of *caveat emptor*: let the buyer beware. Subject to certain statutory exceptions, it is not for the seller to reveal any defects in the goods sold, so that a buyer must be specially alert where the particulars say: 'subject to all faults', or 'as and where lying'. This makes it all the more imperative that a buyer should carry out an investigation for himself and instruct a surveyor to prepare a full report of the yacht and its machinery.

Caveat emptor: let the buyer beware

Private sales

A purchaser may instead of using a broker decide to buy a craft privately; the perils are manifest. The advantages are in cutting out the cost of the agent's commission and VAT, and perhaps of a quicker sale. Private purchase is not a course to be recommended to a novice unless he has experienced aid. A prospective purchaser must take care to confirm that the vendor himself has a good title to transfer. If the boat is registered, the buyer should not content himself with a sight of the Certificate of British Registry, but he should communicate with the Registrar of British Ships at the port at which the boat is registered, to check that it is not subject to a mortgage and that there are no outstanding legal claims attached to the craft. If a mortgage is disclosed, inquiries should be pursued with the mortgagee so that the situation may be resolved.

A seller for his part should satisfy himself that he will get his money. He will therefore in most cases decline to take a cheque save on the condition that the deal will not be regarded as complete, nor the subject-matter transferred, until the cheque banker's draft, or an irrevocable letter of credit.
banker's draft, or an irrevocabl letter of credit.

In a private sale a seller should make a detailed list of such ship's equipment as safety gear, instruments, inflatable and outboard, etc. which he is prepared to include in the asking price, so that no misunderstanding arises on the transfer. This inventory should be checked carefully and agreed on then. It may also serve as a bargaining factor in the course of negotiations as the seller can consent to lower the price but withdraw the listed items which he may, if buying bigger, find useful, or alternatively can dispose of privately by advertisement to his profit.

Bill of Sale

It is the Bill of Sale that completes the sale of a registered British ship, and this can also be used in the case of an unregistered vessel. The official form for this transaction is normally that of a Bill of Sale (Individuals or Joint Owners) as prescribed by the

Commissioner of Customs and Excise with the consent of the Secretary of State for Trade Form No. 10 XS 79 which may be obtained from the Registrar of British Ships (i.e. from the local Customs office and not from HMSO). This sets out the details required which include the official number and name of the ship with the year and port of registry, and whether she be a sailing, steam or motor ship. Details must be entered as to measurement and number of tons and horse power of engine (if any). The form goes on to relate that in consideration of the sum paid, the receipt whereof is hereby acknowledged, the shares in the ship and in her boats and appurtenances are transferred. It certifies that the seller has power to transfer the ship and that such transfer is free from encumbrances, or if there be subsisting encumbrances an endorsement will be made 'save as appears by the registry of the said ship'. The bill is then duly signed in the presence of an ordinary witness whose name and address and description is recorded. Thereafter the instrument is sealed and delivered to the buyer.

A purchaser of a registered ship does not get a complete title until the Bill of Sale has been recorded at the Port of Registry of the ship and neglect of this precaution may entail serious consequences. The transfer or assignment of any ship or vessel, or any share thereof, though by deed as above, and so at first sight a document to which the onerous provisions of the Bills of Sale Acts 1878-1882 would seem to apply, as in fact specifically excluded from the statutory requirements of being filed in the proper form with the Central Office of the Supreme Court.

An additional document to be completed and signed by the buyer is a Declaration by an Individual Owner or Transferee Form No 2 XS 66. This certifies that the seller is a British subject, entitled to 64 shares in the ship, and must be sworn before a Registrar of British ships, a Justice of the Peace, or a Commissioner for Oaths, for which the last mentioned may charge a fee. The declaration may also be made before a British Consular Officer or a solicitor. The Bill of Sale and the declaration of transfer, with the certificate of registry and the statutory fee, is sent to the Registrar at the port of registry.

Deliveries

The buyer of a boat may on completion of the contract be faced with the problem and expense of delivery. This may have been settled under the terms of the agreement, but they may be silent as to this and, where a purchase has been made at a distance, the owner has the task of moving the boat by land or sea. Contact with those engaged in deliveries can be made through recommendations or advertisements, and as with house removal it pays to compare quotations. These may be inclusive of all charges save insurance for the transit; what is expressed to be demurrage may be charged at the rate of £x per day should the vessel be delayed more than 24 hours due to repairs to machinery, hull or gear. All this will remind the new owner to examine his insurance policy, and he for his part may seek to be reimbursed for breakages, or other damage attributable to the deliverer or his crew.

Auctions

Another way of buying a boat is at an auction. Here the sale is complete on the fall of the auctioneer's hammer, or in any other customary manner. Until this any bidder may retract his bid. A sale by auction may be notified as being 'subject to a reserved price' and a right to bid may also be reserved expressly by or on behalf of the seller. Gone are the days when auctions of ships were conducted by inch of candle when the last bid had to be made before the flame was extinguished.

Surveyors

Whether buying new or secondhand the careful purchaser will engage the services of a surveyor. A survey may, in the case of the proposed acquisition of a new craft, reassure the purchaser that he is not receiving a rogue boat off the production line. He also needs to be cautious when being offered a secondhand craft to be sold 'as she lies', as this is proposed with all its faults and not open to survey. In the case of a secondhand vessel, as with house purchase, it is usually courting disaster to dispense with professional advice. Where a buyer later discovered defects, a court has decided that the seller was not liable unless he used artifice to conceal the faults from the buyer. One owner offered his boat for sale 'with all faults'. Knowing that its bottom and keel were rusty, he deliberately took her off the ways after she had been advertised for sale, and floated her in order to conceal her drawbacks. On their subsequent discovery by the purchaser the court ruled that the seller was not liable. A potential purchaser of a houseboat should ensure that the survey includes an examination of the moorings as these usually go with the vessel which may have to take the ground at ebb tide.

Details of experienced marine surveyors and their scale of charges may be had from the Yacht Brokers, Designers and Surveyors Association, or reference may be made to the main surveying institution with global coverage at Lloyd's. The cost of survey is based on the Thames tonnage of the boat, plus travel and subsistence expenses. The surveyor's report is confidential and exclusive to the buyer, who pays for it. A surveyor may be instructed to look at three prospective craft and to select the most favourable for report, or merely to report on one. The surveyor's function is to carry out an extensive examination as to the condition of the craft and its equipment and to report fully. He does not normally purport to deal with the engine in any depth, and hence a marine engineer should be told to carry out this important examination. A surveyor's report can be a persuasive factor in bringing about a reduction in the asking price for the boat; a favourable report may also help to get a marine mortgage. If the report is carelessly prepared so that the client suffers loss, he may have a good claim for damages against the surveyor. For these reasons the surveyor should see that he is adequately protected by a policy of indemnity insurance and he should include an arbitration clause.

Some surveyor's reports have an addendum that the report is a statement of the examination as carried out, and that the surveyor's opinion is given in good faith as to the condition of the structure of the vessel so far as seen, but implies no guarantee and no safeguard against latent or subsequent defects not discovered at the survey. Unless this clause is endorsed by

26

the client at the time of the engagement of the surveyor, the latter cannot thereafter evade his liability to use all proper diligence in preparing his report; according to the YBDSA codebook a report should give an overall assessment of the condition of the boat from which her potential can be deduced.

A surveyor's liability may in certain cases go beyond a duty to his client if he is aware that his report will be seen and acted on by others, unless he effectively excludes his responsibility. As Lord Denning said, when dealing with allegations of negligently compiled accounts which had been shewn by the clients for whom they had been prepared to a prospective investor who was influenced thereby to put £2000 into the business which he lost: 'I say that a duty to use care in making a statement does exist apart from a contract in that behalf. First what persons are under such duty? My answer is those persons such as accountants, surveyors, valuers and analysts, whose profession and occupation is to examine books, accounts and other things and to make reports on which other people, other than their clients, rely in the ordinary course of business. Their duty is not only to use care in their reports, they have also a duty to use care in their work which results in their reports. Secondly to whom do these professional people owe the duty? They owe the duty to their employer, or client, and also I think to any third person to whom they themselves show the accounts, or to whom they know their employer is going to show the accounts, so as to induce him to invest money or take some other action on them. Thirdly to what transactions does the duty of care extend? It extends I think to any of those transactions for which the accountants knew their accounts were required'.

A Lloyd's surveyor who, in surveying for classification purposes, negligently passes a mast as sound when it is not, is not liable to the owner for damage caused by its breaking; the surveyor makes his report only for the object of classifying the ship for the Yacht Register and not otherwise.

Unfair Contract Terms Act

Attempts are sometimes made by sellers of goods, or suppliers of services, to exclude themselves by notices or printed terms from legal liability for negligence and for breach of contractual conditions, warranties or other undertakings. The Unfair Contract Terms Act 1977 is designed to meet abuses by such exemptions. A person cannot by reference to any contract terms, or notice, exclude or restrict his liability for death or personal injury resulting from negligence. In the case of other loss or damage a person cannot opt out from liability for negligence if it would be unreasonable to do so. Similarly where a consumer contracts to acquire goods under written standard terms of business, the seller's contractual liability cannot be excluded or restricted save in so far as this be fair and reasonable paying regard to the circumstances which were or ought reasonably to have been known to, or in contemplation of the parties when the contract was made.

Marine mortgage

Finance is a dominating factor when buying a boat. How is this to be raised? Is the cost to come out of capital or will there be a need to approach the bank manager for a loan? A consideration in raising the necessary finance depends on whether the boat is registered or not. In the main the former may attract a marine mortgage, whereas the latter points towards hire-purchase, or a personal loan. The terms of marine mortgage are a matter for individual negotiation. It may usually be taken that registration is a condition of the granting of an advance. In general, advances are made up to 80% on new craft, and up to 75% on secondhand boats, with a maximum repayment period of 5 to 10 years. The terms may be 30% deposit on order made subject to contract; 40% on completion of mouldings less deposit; balance on completion of the boat but before delivery. There should be produced a current dry survey report and an expert valuation. Moreover a policy of insurance must be effected affording comprehensive cover and to include third parties. Interest rates may be expressed to be either on a flat interest rate, or at a rate linked to the Finance Houses Association's base rate. A bank loan may be at the actual rate of interest payable on the balance outstanding, or it may be on a flat rate basis, so that the borrower will have to continue to pay the same amount of interest throughout despite sums already paid.

A borrower will be wary of seeking to raise a loan other than from reputable financial dealers. The Consumer Credit Act 1974 gives the courts power to grant relief to those who have entered into extortionate credit transactions where the terms insist on grossly exorbitant payments, or which blatantly breach the ordinary principles of fair dealing. A court has wide powers which include setting such agreements aside or ordering the repayment of unreasonable interest charges. Those seeking to raise the wind should steer clear of entering into such a dubious transaction in the first instance. They would do well to recall the apocryphal story which is told of the financier who fell overboard on the high seas to the intense interest of an attendant shark. It was the fear of all that he would make short work of his quarry. Not a bit of it. He just rubbed noses and swam off. 'What a splendid example of professional etiquette', exclaimed an onlooker.

A request for a mortgage is made by completing a proposal form giving details as to:

(a) private address and whether this is occupied as owner or tenant;
(b) occupation and business address and nature of business and of its capital or turnover;
(c) particulars of the vessel, price and amount of loan wanted;
(d) proposed repayment periods and the instalments by which the loan is to be discharged;
(e) name of bankers and insurers;
(f) an up to date survey report.

Under the 1894 Act, a registered ship or a share therein may be made a security for a loan which ranks as a mortgage. This must be made along the lines set out in the statute and is produced to the registrar of the port of registry where it is recorded in the register book. Where a registered mortgage is discharged, the registrar, on production of the mortgage deed with a receipt for the mortgage money endorsed thereon duly signed and attested, must make an entry in the register to the effect that the mortgage has been discharged. There are also provisions applicable to the transfer of a mortgage and as to the transmission of any interest on death, bankruptcy, marriage or by any lawful means. By the Merchant Shipping (Fees) Regulations, charges are prescribed in connection with the recording of mortgages, as also for the inspection of the register. If this is effected through the services of a professional agent, additional expenses will be incurred.

Any person buying a registered boat should cause a search of the Register and so satisfy himself by such inspection that the vessel is clear of all charges. A seller for his part should appreciate that some additional fee will be payable by him for ensuring that the registered record shows the discharge of all outstanding encumbrances.

Hire-purchase

Finance for an unregistered yacht may be arranged by hire-purchase or credit-sale agreement, or by loan. A hire-purchase agreement is one under which the owner in whom the yacht is vested lets it out on hire and agrees that the hirer may either return the boat and terminate the hiring, or that he may elect to exercise an option to purchase it after the agreed amount has been paid. Credit-sales are similar to hire-purchase transactions, with the difference that the goods are vested in an individual and then paid for by instalments. The Consumer Credit Act 1974 applies where a sale is made on credit terms to an individual and the credit is below the ceiling figure currently prescribed.

Where a boat is acquired on credit the client has to sign a credit order form and to make a down payment plus VAT on the cash price, and agree to pay the balance in so many monthly instalments at a fixed sum. He must, if he signs the agreement otherwise than on trade premises, be told of his right to cancel: 'You have, for a short time, a legal right to cancel this agreement. You can do this in writing, saying that you are cancelling the agreement to the X firm at the Y address. You must post your letter before the end of the third day after the day on which you receive your copy of the agreement. If you do cancel this agreement, any money you have already paid will be returned to you'. If the hirer defaults in his payments the craft may be re-possessed by the hiree. Until all payments are made the hirer is not the owner. Until he completes the stipulated instalments he cannot sell the boat for he has no good title to transmit.

Not infrequently, and especially if the prospective purchaser be under age, a guarantor is required. A guarantor should be aware of his obligations under the law, which enable the seller to recoup from him in the event of any default. The golden rule at law is:

(a) read the small print;
(b) think before signing.

Bank loan

Probably, short of an interest-free offer of credit by a trader, there is no cheaper and safer way of raising the cash than by a bank loan. Perhaps a simple overdraft facility will be enough; or it may be that a personal loan is indicated. In the case of the latter the bank will need to be satisfied that the borrower is over 18 years of age and is credit-worthy. He will be expected to make some contribution to the cost of the purchase itself and recommended to take out insurance cover against unemployment, illness, accident or death. He will be quoted the terms of instalment payments both as to time and amounts and APR. He should observe that one of the terms to which he puts his signature is normally to the effect that he agrees that the total amount, less any already paid, will become immediately repayable on demand if any instalment is not met on the due date, or if the bank at any time in its discretion considers the loan to be at risk. Once the loan is sanctioned he is free to buy the boat outright. He is the owner, not the bank. In effect the transaction is an unsecured loan repayable by instalments. In some loaning arrangements, however, a bank may insist on some security such as the deposit of the title deeds to a home, or the naming of a guarantor.

Sharing

The escalating cost of buying and maintaining a boat has led to many entering into sharing or syndicate arrangements. If such an arrangement is for the purpose of carrying on a business in common for profit, the Partnership Act 1890, unless excluded, will obtain. Even where no business is run, the 1890 Act (which records the common law and equitable rules on joint ownership) is a useful measure to which associates should refer for guidance.

Although there is no legal need for any sharing arrangement to be put in writing, it is most advisable that a formal document is drafted as to sharing and management along the lines suggested by RYA. This is a situation where, though the understanding may be as between friends, nevertheless proper legal formalities should be observed in the interests of all. The paths to the law courts are littered with broken gentlemen's agreements.

The contract should recite the names of the parties and proceed to apportion the shares to be held, expressed as a proportion of 64. There is no limit on the number of co-owners who may join, but not more than five may be entered as registered owners; the agreement should vest the managerial position in one of the nominated owners to be responsible for the daily routine decisions, as also, after consultation with his associates, in dealing with more extensive matters. The object of the enterprise should be set forth, as for instance whether it is limited to racing and cruising, or extends to chartering and other activities. If chartering is a main aim, then the rules of the Partnership Act 1890 may apply.

The contract should specify the subject-matter, namely the boat, equipment and gear, with a full inventory attached by way of schedule. Although the dissolution of the syndicate is the last matter which the associates will have in mind at the start of the venture, provision should be made for the appropriate means of bringing it to an end. The method of serving notice of termination, normally contemplated as 6 months, should be recited as also the ensuing liabilities. The procedure to be followed in the event of the death of a co-owner should be outlined, as also the rules to be adopted should a co-owner wish to assign or transfer his share. It should be spelt out that no further person is to be introduced as a partner without the consent of all the others. Terms should be included for the disposal of the yacht and for the division of the proceeds on the ending of the syndicate. This could allow for the disposal of the boat through a broker, or by public auction. A right may be reserved for any of the owners to be free to acquire the boat, and it should be said whether this is to be at a figure based on the price paid or on a valuation at the material date.

Plainly any deed should mirror the financial arrangements between the parties. A bank account should be opened in the names of the co-owners, rules fixed as to payments in and takings out, and as to casual disbursements. A clause should allow for proper accounts to be kept and for their annual audit. In practice there will doubtless be many problems which the agreement in retrospect will be powerless to resolve. Nevertheless all efforts should be made to set out in black and white the demarcation lines of financial responsibility, even down to such fine points as provisioning the galley or funding the ship's petty cash purse.

A ship cannot go to sea with a multiplicity of skippers, so authority needs to be vested in one individual to supervise the management and use of the craft; his duties should be listed. It should be made clear that after due consultation he may put in hand necessary repairs to the yacht, sails, engine, gear etc; he should be made responsible for insuring the vessel. To him will be left the duty of conducting the ship's business as to shipyards, chandlers, sail-loft, mooring or marina dues. It will fall to him to deal with any legal or salvage claims, and he should insist that he be indemnified on that account.

Finally the agreement should relate the procedure for resolving disputes. It is a principle of partnership that any difference as to ordinary matters connected with the venture may be decided by a majority of the partners, but no change may be made in its nature without the consent of all. In the event of irreconcilable differences, an arbitration clause should be included so that there may be an independent adjudication.

Charter

Many have started their sailing career by hiring a craft and have then graduated into buying their own, making the boat pay her way by charter. This an owner can do himself by private introduction or public advertisement, or by relying on an experienced agency. Whether thoughts of hiring rove from family fun aboard a cruiser on the Norfolk Broads, to the fascination of joining a flotilla fleet in the Caribbean, or letting out a yacht for sailing inland or offshore, there should be an awareness as to the practical and legal problems which can arise. An arrangement for hiring may be made by word of mouth, or in writing contained in correspondence, or by charterparty.

A contract by charterparty is an agreement by which a vessel is let out to another party on terms. It may be a bareboat or supervised charter. In the former the charterer assumes full control of the boat; in the latter the owner maintains command. In a self-sail situation there is an implied term that the hirer is a competent skipper able to handle the craft of his choice. On the other side of the coin there is an implied term that the ship let out shall be tight, staunch and as fit for the purpose as reasonable care can make her.

One way to effect a successful charter is to deal with a member of a recognised charter or travel organisation such as the Yacht Charter Association Ltd, Associated Scottish Yacht Charters, or those with approved standards, i.e. IATA licence, ATOL number, ABTA membership. Excellent arrangements can, of course, be made through other reputable charterers but all care should be taken to avoid falling prey to the odd unscrupulous shark in the trade as was once the fate of a family who hired a launch on the Thames. Off Sonning it went up in flames. The fire extinguisher and sand box were empty. They jumped ashore. They claimed damages for burns, bruises and loss of kit. The owner argued that there was no undertaking on his part as to the fitness of the craft and that it was not incumbent upon him to supply an efficient extinguisher. The trial judge ruled in favour of the family. He said that there was a presumption that the launch was not reasonably fit for the purpose for which she was let.

The Yacht Charter Association formed in 1960 acts on behalf of its UK members who carry on a *bona fide* sea-going charter business with locations covering the British Isles. It advises its members on matters of safety, seaworthiness and the law. It insists on a high standard as to boat and gear and as to courtesy, cleanliness, service and insurance which is liable to be confirmed by inspection. It has, with the approval of the British Tourist Authority, introduced a register of British charter yachts on which single boat owners can be included provided that they comply with the stringent requirements and pay the requisite fee. The YCA has the advantage of being able to offer coast-wide reciprocal aid as to service, spares and repairs.

Charter procedure

Most charters come about as the result of an advertisement such as in the *Yachting Monthly*'s annual *Charter Guide,* or as the result of a recommendation leading to a request for a brochure or other particulars. This will bring a reply indicating, *inter alia,* availability, cost inclusive of VAT, and a booking form along with the terms of letting. These will normally indicate that a 25% deposit of the cost is payable on booking and the balance 14 days before the start of the charter in respect of which a full agreement is required to be signed. The agreement may be cancelled before signing when the deposit will be returned in full. After signing it may be cancelled up to 2 months from the agreed date with loss of the deposit; thereafter the hiree is stated to be liable in full.

Security deposit

A deposit signifies that the hirer is in earnest and ranks as security to the hiree. If all goes to plan it is credited to the account. If the hirer defaults then it is generally forfeit. There are circumstances in which the hiree makes a further letting and incurs no loss when it can be argued that any amount claimed over and above his administrative charges and inconvenience may be by way of unreasonable penalty and thus recoverable by the hirer. However, if a booking is broken and the gap after all reasonable endeavours cannot be made good, the total loss falls on the hirer minus such deductions as to unconsumed fuel, gas, rations, etc. and some sum may perhaps be apportioned as to the saving of the wear and tear of the boat.

A further security deposit of £200 is payable 14 days before the start of the charter period subject to a refund within 14 days of the letting, less the cost of any uninsured damage, loss or other liabilities. In this context a specific scrutiny should be made of the inventory on joining and leaving ship.

A hirer should not only as a matter of contract but of honour report all known losses and damage, and hand a clean boat back at 1000 hours on the last day, in default of which a cleaning charge of £25 may be made. Chartered boats normally set off with full fuel, water and gas supplies and must be returned in a similar state on takeover.

Delay

In chartering, time is very much of the essence of the exercise. The hirer expects to collect the boat at a set time and place and similarly undertakes to return it. If storm bound cross channel and he cannot keep to the timetable he will have to pay for the delay. In the event of a delay in handover at the start of the charter a *pro rata* refund may be made for every 12 hours. If the yacht is not returned on time a *pro rata* charge will be made at twice the weekly rate. Furthermore if the yacht is not returned to the stipulated port a charge may be made for the expenses of collection, and delivery fees being what they are these may be considerable.

Charterparty

On receipt of the booking form the applicant, if he wants to go ahead, will state whether he wishes to sail himself or be skippered. If a bareboat is requested he will be required to provide bank and sailing references and to indicate his intended itinerary. He will then get a charter agreement which he should read, mark and inwardly digest. In particular he should read what matters are covered by insurance and what are not and take out any additional cover to safeguard his personal position. One of the matters which a charterer should consider when booking is the possibility of cancellation arising through illness, accident or other cause, e.g. jury service. He marks his cruising limits which are set out, such as Cherbourg to La Coruña, and any other restrictions which may be imposed such

36

as to racing, towing or operating after dark in inland waters, or permitting any minor to operate the boat save under experienced adult supervision. He should digest the fact that in the event of any dispute which cannot be settled amicably that there is an arbitration clause. One such clause undertakes to refer disputes to a nominee appointed by the RYA; another to two arbitrators to be appointed by each party. This procedure is designed to provide for a simple and inexpensive method of investigation which can take the form of the examination of documents and not of parties.

A good example of the approach which a court may make as to the measure of damages to be applied in the event of a craft wrongfully colliding with another kept for charter is illustrated by the case of *The Fortunity*. She rammed and sank the *Four of Hearts* on the Norfolk Broads which was one of a class of 13 motor cruisers available for hire. She was a popular craft of distinctive design and character. Her owners wished for a similar replacement. This took time to arrange and led to loss of profits on a season's bookings. A court awarded damages to cover the market value of the cruiser plus loss of profits for the season which could fairly be fixed by comparison with other hirings of similar craft by the same owners. The basis for the decision was that the measure of damage is the value of a ship to her owner as a going concern at the time and place of her loss.

Registration

Under Part 1 of the Merchant Shipping Act 1894, every boat over 15 tons is required to be officially registered, but pleasure boats not exceeding 15 tons burden (net) used for navigation, and not propelled by oars, whose activities are confined to the rivers and coasts of the UK, do not require to be formally registered under the Merchant Shipping Acts and are exempt from compulsory pilotage. Yachts, however, engaged in fishing at sea need to be registered as fishing boats. The Register of British ships is kept by the Department of Trade, who will supply Merchant Shipping Notice M 1030 describing the procedure to be followed by owners and builders of pleasure yachts of under 13.7 metres (45 feet) overall length. A British owned pleasure yacht is defined as one which is owned wholly by British subjects, or bodies corporate. Although an alien cannot so register, there is nothing to prevent him from forming a so styled 'one man company' which may then be registered as the owner.

Registration has become an increasingly expensive process. It can be done by the owner himself, or through the services of an agent. If an owner does decide to do it himself, he will find the authorities most helpful in guiding him through the complicated procedure. The advantages of registration are that it provides proper evidence of title and facilitates the transfer of the craft when it comes to a sale. It enables a yacht to go foreign with internationally recognised papers to identify it as a British ship, and it confers all the privileges of the British flag. It assists with any communications which may be necessary with British consular officials in matters of a civil, and even of a criminal nature. It is almost invariably required when a mortgage is sought. Registration also assists an owner seeking an Admiralty warrant to wear a privileged ensign. In the event of any claim calling for assessment by tonnage, or for a demand for harbour dues based upon measurement, registration constitutes conclusive evidence; it also helps in establishing an entitlement to carry bonded stores. The disadvantages of registration lie not only in the cost of completing the formalities, but in marking the boat, and time and trouble, often extending over 3 months.

A ship is traditionally divided into 64 shares. A maximum of 64 may be registered as owners but as has already been explained, the number of joint owners, as in a syndicate, is limited to five. Any seeming contradiction here is resolved by section 5 of the 1894 Act which makes a distinction between individual ownership of shares and the collective ownership thereof; in the case of the latter there is a restriction on numbers and on functions.

Application

The first step towards registration is taken by the owner applying to the Registrar of British ships at the Customs and Excise office at an approved port in England, Wales, the

Channel Islands, Isle of Man, Scotland or Northern Ireland. The London Registrar is at Custom House, Lower Thames Street, EC3, and further information may be had from the Registrar-General of Shipping and Seamen at the Department of Trade in Cardiff. The owner simply needs to write to any port of his choice (it need not necessarily be his home port) requesting that he be registered at such port and stating that he is a member of a yacht club. If an agent is authorised to make the application on the owner's behalf, then an authority from the owner for the agent to act must be enclosed.

Name

An application must next be made to the Registrar General for the approval of the yacht's name. Three names should be submitted in case the first two are refused. In general, the owner of an *unregistered* yacht may sail under any name he likes, provided that the use of such name is not for fraudulent purposes, and that it does not offend against the trade protection rules of 'passing off'.

It is not unusual for the registered owner of a yacht named, say, *D D I* to wish his replacement craft to be called *D D II* and so on. In the result, this constitutes a change of name which looks as if it so closely resembles the name of an existing ship as to incur the disapproval of the Registrar of British Ships. Certain discretionary leeway in these circumstances may be exercised by the Registrar General if he is satisfied that the craft is the replacement for another formerly owned by the applicant; the alteration is but numerical, and the craft will operate only from a port or harbour where no other ship of the same name is designated; or in exceptional cases of emergency a deposit is paid, and an undertaking given to change the name within a year to such as may be approved. In the final analysis the discretion of the Registrar as to approval of a name is paramount.

In selecting a name an owner was formerly assisted by Lloyd's comprehensive *Register of Yachts* which has now been discontinued. Short of inspecting the official Register for a fee, a reference to the new *Debrett's Register of Yachts* may give some guidance as to nomenclature. For launches (i.e. any mechanically propelled vessels) which may be used on the freshwater Thames beyond Teddington applicants should ascertain from Thames Water, prior to registry, if the proposed name is acceptable.

Several names should be submitted . . .

If the proposed name does not appear already as the name of a registered British ship, or if it is not so similar to that of such a ship as to be calculated to deceive, the Registrar will give his certificate of approval. If subsequent to registration the owner wishes to change the name of his craft, he must give notice to the Registrar and seek his approval. This may entail him inserting an official advertisement in stipulated publications that: 'in consequence of personal preference', or 'in consequence of an agreement with the previous owner', or whatever the case may be, application has been made to change the name of the ship and all objections should be communicated to the Registrar General within seven days.

In general sympathetic consideration is given to any proposed harmless modification of an existing name such as *DD of Ballyholme* or *Grey DD*.

An owner when selling his boat to get another, should safeguard any wish to transfer the name to his new boat by making it a term of the contract that the buyer will undertake to change the name of the old.

Declaration of ownership

The owner must now prove his title to the vessel. This he may do if he is the first owner, by producing the builder's certificate supported by a declaration of ownership. The builder's certificate states that the boat was built at their yard, and sets out particulars as to sail, steam or motor as also length, breadth, depth, tonnage, with details of the engine, if any; if the builder is a limited company, the certificate must be given under the seal of the company. When the applicant is not the first owner, he must in addition produce documentary evidence as to all previous changes of ownership in continuous line from the first owner, which will be the respective Bills of Sale. The Declaration of Ownership must be sworn before a Registrar of British ships, a Justice of the Peace, a Commissioner of Oaths (who may make a charge), or a British Consular officer; it certifies that the applicant is a British subject and that the general description of the ship is correct, and declares: 'I am entitled to be registered as owner of 64 shares in the ship. To the best of my knowledge and belief no person or body of persons is entitled to any interest whatever either legal or beneficial in the said ship'.

Survey

The yacht will have to be surveyed. For vessels under 13.7 metres (45 feet), application for the measurement for tonnage of the yacht and the issue of a certificate of survey (tonnage measurement) may be made to Lloyd's Register of Shipping, Yacht and Small Craft Department, Southampton, or to the RYA or YBDSA. This sets out the particulars of the yacht and the place, date and time where it can be seen. The measurement of a pleasure yacht for tonnage purposes, and the issue of a certificate of survey, must not be regarded as signifying that the yacht has been inspected for seaworthiness, structural strength or condition.

The owner must arrange for someone to be in attendance at the time of the survey, and he will be required to pay the prescribed fees. If the surveyor makes an abortive visit because the boat is not accessible, the owner will be liable for extra charges. Any subsequent alteration to the craft may call for a further survey. Particulars of any engine must be certified by the owner, builder or engine manufacturer.

Carving

When the Registrar is satisfied that the survey requirements have been met, he issues a carving and marking note to the owner. This now requires him to mark out on the main beam, or (in the case of fibreglass, etc) as otherwise directed, the registered tons accompanied by the official number, and indicating if the name and port of registry are to be permanently marked on the stern (members of certain yacht clubs are exempt). Samuel Plimsoll was responsible for the introduction of the Load or Plimsoll Line which applies to British ships of 80 tons and over, but pleasure yachts and vessels engaged in fishing are exempt.

Certificate of registry

Finally on payment of the registry fee at the office of HM Customs and Excise, the Registrar will register the yacht and issue a certificate which should be kept with the ship's papers. The form records the particulars of the vessel, its official number, name and port of registry. It sets out the builders, dimensions and engine. It lists the name, residence and occupation of the owner and the number of the shares held. It gives notice that a certificate of registration is not a document of title. It does not necessarily contain notice of all changes of ownership, and in no case does it show an official record of any mortgages affecting the ship. All changes of ownership, address or other registered particulars should be notified to the Registrar. Registration of a yacht does not in itself establish title to its duty free re-admission into the UK. Details of any change of a registered yacht are communicated to the Inland Revenue.

Small ships register

An alternative method of registration to Part 1 of the 1894 Act is available under the Merchant Shipping Act 1983 whereby a small ship may, instead of having her tonnage ascertained, be measured for length. Section 10 defines a small ship as less than 24 metres (79 feet). This includes yachts, motor boats and inflatables but not fishing vessels, submersibles or pleasure craft owned by companies. Owners wishing to apply for a Certificate of Registry on the Small Ships Register do so to the RYA who act on behalf of the Department of Transport. The SSR scheme is significantly cheaper and less complicated than the Part 1 procedure. The certificate establishes the British nationality of a boat. By law there is an obligation to register a ship before taking her into international waters or to foreign countries. By international law these are entitled to require evidence of the nationality of a visiting vessel. It should be appreciated that an SSR certificate does not constitute *prima facie* legal title to the ownership of a ship, nor does the register afford a means of recording legal mortgages. Hence only Part 1 offers effective cover as to this.

Application to be included on the SSR must be made on the form obtainable from the RYA setting out the details of the ship, overall length in metres to the nearest centimetre (the owner may measure himself) and name. Undesirable names will not be accepted. Particulars of the owner(s) must be supplied. They must be Commonwealth citizens ordinarily resident in the United Kingdom. It is a criminal offence to make a false declaration, or to misuse a certificate, or to fail to ensure that the requirement of marking is met, and to fail to surrender the certificate on expiry. However it is a defence for a person charged with such breach to prove that he took all reasonable precautions and exercised all due diligence.

If the application is in order then on payment of a registration fee of £10 a Certificate of Registry valid for 5 years (and renewable thereafter) will be issued. The craft must then be marked with the alloted number on a plaque with painted letters SSR on an exterior surface where it will be plainly visible.

Flags

Once his boat is registered, the owner should look to his colours. Under the 1894 Act he must at all times have the red ensign aboard. All British ships, registered or unregistered are entitled – and indeed required, at certain times – to wear the red ensign. It is an offence for a private pleasure yacht to wear the Union Jack, or flag, as this is reserved for Royalty and the Royal Navy.

The red ensign usually worn by merchant ships without any defacement is the proper national colours for all British ships, except in the case of HM ships, or those allowed to wear any other national colours in pursuance of a warrant from Her Majesty.

A ship belonging to a British subject shall hoist the proper national colours:

(a) on a signal made to her by one of HM ships; and
(b) on entering or leaving any foreign port.

Section 9 of the Merchant Shipping Act 1983 exempts those on the SSR from section 74 of the 1894 Act which requires ships of 50 tons or more to show proper national colours on entering or leaving any British port.

Special Ensigns

By Ministry of Defence warrant, members of certain yacht clubs are accorded the privilege of wearing special Ensigns; the white Ensign is reserved to the Royal Yacht Squadron; the undefaced Blue Ensign to members of some clubs; the defaced blue or red Ensign to certain others. The fact that a yacht of the RYS is authorised to fly the white Ensign does not confer on her the status of one of HM ships.

Prior to April 1985 registration under Part 1 was a condition precedent to the grant of an MOD warrant. Since then eligibility has been extended to yachts entered on the SSR.

Warrants issued before April 1985 stay valid until a boat is sold and may be retained thereafter as a souvenir. Company-owned yachts cannot be included on the SSR but may qualify if registered under Part 1 provided that they are not used for professional, business or commercial purposes and so long as the name does not incorporate a name, product or trade mark used for business or commercial aims.

There are about 1500 yacht clubs in the UK and Channel Islands of which but 70 or so are entitled clubs as set out in the Navy List. Members of entitled clubs are able to apply through them for the privilege of wearing a special Ensign. The RYA acts as agents for the MOD in the printing and supply of the permits and deals with the requisite annual returns as directed by the Admiralty board.

A warrant from the MOD confers on the Flag Officers and Committees the ability to issue permits at a nominal cost to their members to wear, on yachts owned or chartered by them, the Ensign of Her Majesty's Fleet with the distinctive marks of the club thereon subject to the following conditions.

To qualify, the yacht must be registered under Part 1 of the 1894 Act; or be on the SSR. The yacht must not measure less than 2 tons gross if registered by tonnage; or 7 metres in length overall if registered by length. The permit is personal to the owner and is vested in him alone. The Ensign can only be flown when he is on board or in effective control of the yacht while near at hand on shore; it may also be flown from the yacht's tender. The warrant should be kept aboard with the ship's papers failing which the Ensign may not be worn. The Royal Navy is empowered to stop any vessel wearing privileged colours and to ask for proof of authority. The permit must be returned on cessation of membership or ownership.

When cruising in foreign waters care must be taken to avoid any action which would result in complications with a foreign power. Those intending to sail in foreign waters affected by war or serious disturbance should notify the MOD. Owners should also note that it is naval etiquette when in harbour to hoist the Ensign at 0800 hours (0900 between 1st November and 14th February) and to lower it at sunset (or at 2100 local time if earlier). The penalty for the improper wearing of the Union

45

Flag, the White Ensign, Blue Ensign (plain or defaced) and the Red Ensign with any defacement is £1000. Holders of MOD permits are allowed the benefit of mooring at government buoys, and at naval dockyard ports in the UK, as a matter of courtesy and at the discretion of the harbour master.

An owner must ensure that the Ensign is only flown with the burgee of the yacht club through which the permit was granted for this symbolises that the yacht belongs to a listed club and is commissioned for cruising.

3 Insurance

This the Baker suggested, and offered for hire
(On moderate terms), or for sale,
Two excellent Policies, one against Fire
And one against damage from Hail.
                              Lewis Carroll
                    'The Hunting of the Snark'

Marine insurance

Insurance of a yacht against third party risks is not compulsory as it is with vehicles under the Road Traffic Acts, but indirectly it may be so, because certain public harbour authorities, as also private marina concerns, may make the grant of a mooring or berth conditional on this; a finance house advancing a marine mortgage, or loan, may also insist on such security.

The first known marine policy in England was in 1555. By the end of the 17th century this insurance, which had formerly been carried out by bankers, came to be transacted at the fashionable coffee house of Edward Lloyd. Today the underwriting business at Lloyd's is carried on by some 26 000 members. The first move in taking out an insurance of a craft at Lloyd's, or elsewhere, is to approach a marine broker who is responsible for negotiating the transaction with the underwriters. A contract of insurance is an agreement whereby one party (the 'insurer') promises in return for a money consideration (the 'premium') to pay to the other party (the 'assured') a sum of money, or provide him with some corresponding benefit, upon the occurrence of one or more specified events. The onus is on an assured to show that on a balance of probabilities the loss or event was effectively caused by the perils covered.

In marine insurance one party for a stated sum undertakes to indemnify the other against loss arising from perils of the sea. The law here is codified in the Marine Insurance Act 1906 which defines this as a contract of indemnity against losses incident to marine adventures accruing to the ship, cargo, freight or other subject matter of a policy during a given voyage or voyages, or during a given length of time. It sets out in archaic language the basic cover:

'BE IT KNOWN THAT: touching the adventures and perils which we the assurers, are contented to bear and do take upon us in this voyage: they are of the seas, men-of-war, fire, enemies, pirates, rovers, thieves, jettisons, letters of mart and counter-mart, surprisals, takings at sea, arrests, restraints and detainment of all Kings, princes and people ...'

It is not surprising that judicial comments on this form of policy have been that it is ungrammatical and obscure and, without the aid of usage and of legal decisions, unintelligible. Fortunately the Act lays down canons of construction, and court rulings accord with the accepted customs of the seas.

Insurable interest

An owner must show that he has an insurable interest. The

Notify the insurance company as soon as possible

precise terms of the policy may be negotiated, and he asks for cover by making a proposal which, if accepted, is expressed in terms of a policy for which a premium is paid. Before making a proposal the owner should call for a specimen policy and read it with care, including the small print, and compare it with others. Once the premium is paid the relationship of insurer and insured is created. The standardised version is that set out in the schedule to the 1906 Act to which, since the 1920s, there have been added the Institute Yacht Clauses.

The standard Lloyd's and Institute Yacht Clauses policies state what perils are covered; all else is excluded. Alternative yacht policies may offer a wider cover accepting all risks, and excluding only those which are specifically named as exclusions. In the insurance market, as elsewhere, it pays to shop around, bearing in mind that an owner only gets ultimately for what he pays. The true test of the efficacy of cover is when a claim is made. An owner should heed the caution given by the Insurance Ombudsman Bureau in their first annual report: 'Every word of an insurance policy is put there for a purpose. If the purpose is not clear get sound advice, preferably before the policy is bought'.

Proposal form

The contract of insurance originates from a written proposal made by the yachtsman. He states on a form his name and address and details of the type and class of his craft, and whether it is moored or berthed. A declaration is made as to the period of cover, and as to the dates when the yacht is to be in commission and when laid up ashore or elsewhere. This reflects in assessing the premium, as does a statement as to the cruising range. An owner should be mindful of his effective range of cover when cruising. A catamaran was insured under a policy which protected her whilst she was 'within the United Kingdom either ashore or afloat'. She was damaged on a passage from the west country to the Channel Islands. The appeal court decided that the craft was uncovered, as the Channel Islands were not part of the United Kingdom.

The owner places a valuation on his craft and equipment,

49

dealing with such navigational aids as DF, RT and radar; he also states whether he wishes to include such items as dinghy, outboard and liferaft. He should consider if he wants cover for his personal effects, or for a trailer or trolley, or other special equipment. He also sets out any excess that he is prepared to accept in the event of a claim; in other words what initial part of any claim he is prepared to pay himself; the larger this amount the lower will be his premium.

Sometimes searching questions as to safety and security are asked. The owner may be requested to state his sailing qualifications and also those of anyone else who may regularly take the helm. He may be required to furnish a history of the mooring. He may have to declare whether his yacht is fitted with log, distress flares, additional chain or warps. He may have further to deal with the security arrangements as to the tender and its outboard. Premiums are assessed on local reputation. Abersoch, with Holyhead a close second, are alleged to suffer the most serious loss ratio of all moorings in the UK, and to be disaster areas as to vandalism, theft and freak conditions.

Duty of disclosure

A contract of insurance differs from ordinary forms of contract, especially in the duty of disclosure. When selling a boat the transaction is basically one of *caveat emptor* (buyer beware). It is not for the seller to decry his own wares, and he is under no duty to speak up. He is entitled to leave it to the buyer to carry out an inspection for himself. However, in the case of insurance there is a duty on the owner to make full disclosure. An insurance contract is said to be one of *uberrimae fidei* i.e. of the utmost good faith. To fail to be frank may be fatal to the validity of the policy. A false answer to a question, or a lack of candour, may render the contract voidable at the option of the insurance company. It is for the insured to supply information of all material facts of which he is aware, or ought to be aware, in order to enable a prudent insurer to assess fairly the risks to be assumed. Under the 1906 Act every circumsance is material, which would influence the judgment of a prudent insurer in fixing the premium or determining whether he will take the risk.

Over and above completing any questionnaire and certifying its accuracy there is a duty to disclose, if needs be, matters not specifically raised therein. As a judge once explained: 'Now, insurance is a contract of the utmost good faith and it is of the gravest importance to commerce that this position should be observed. The underwriter knows nothing of the particular circumstances of the voyage to be insured. The assured knows a great deal. It is the duty of the assured to inform the underwriter of everything that he is not taken as knowing, so that the contract may be entered into on an equal footing'.

A proposer may be asked to sign a declaration that the boat is to be used solely for private and pleasure purposes and not let out for hire, charter or reward. He may also be called on to certify that neither he nor anyone likely to use the boat has been refused insurance before. The proposer may also be required to state that if the form is completed in writing other than his own, that the author thereof is his agent.

Completion of a questionnaire, and the signing of any declaration that it shall form the basis of any contract of insurance between the owner and the underwriter, do not create an irrevocable relationship, because an owner is free to accept or to reject the final quotation offered. Any failure to disclose any matter of significance, or the making of a misstatement by the assured, enables the insurer to declare the policy to be null and void, and the premium paid to be forfeit. In a 1983 case an owner who had amateur built a sloop insured it for £15 000. In his proposal form he failed to mention this and also that he had once been convicted for handling a stolen dinghy. The yacht was lost at sea. The insurers successfully rejected his claim on the grounds that he had neglected to inform them of material facts. The duty of disclosure is a continuing one and accordingly care should be taken to communicate any material change in circumstances which may occur during the currency of the policy.

Valuation

An early calculation to be made by an owner is the value of his craft. He should avoid any exaggeration of its worth, but allow

51

for inflationary factors. If the value of his interest exceeds the sum insured, the excess of interest is uncovered by the policy and he is his own insurer as to the uninsured balance. To overinsure is no profit, for he is deemed to have made a present of the additional premium to the insurer. What he should do is to declare the valuation of the vessel to be that prevailing in the current state of the market, to which the yachting press is a good guide, for that alone will be the maximum amount which may be recovered.

Personal effects

If it is wished to safeguard personal effects not already covered by a domestic policy, there should be a separate arrangement. This cover may extend to the belongings of the assured and his family whilst afloat, or whilst in transit to or from the craft. Who are members of the family? In broad terms all those of common stock i.e. blood relations. What are personal effects? They have been judicially defined to be any used portable articles on the person of a seaman which he might reasonably be expected to carry with him for his own regular and private use, and includes clothing. Some insurers make it clear that the personal effects clause does not apply to radios, TV sets, tape recorders, cameras and watches, for which a separate All Risks extension should be sought. Normally articles such as cash, drink, jewellery and objets d'art are also excluded. It is common for a maximum limit to be fixed in respect of the loss of any one item. In general, wider and cheaper cover is to be got under the All Risks section of a Household Policy.

Total and partial loss

Under the 1906 Act a loss may be either total or partial. Any loss other than a total loss is a partial loss. A total loss may be either an actual total loss or a constructive total loss. A constructive total loss occurs where the cost of salvaging and repairing a wrecked vessel would exceed her value when repaired. A policy may provide that in assessing whether the craft is a constructive total loss, the insured value should be taken to be the repaired value. Actual total loss happens where the craft is so destroyed or damaged as to cease to be a thing of the kind insured, or where the assured is irretrievably deprived of it. In the event of total loss of the vessel, the assured is required to abandon his interest in her to the insurer from whom he recovers. In one case where a ship sank, the insurers raised her at vast cost and then asserted that, as she could be repaired for less than her value, the loss was only partial. It was held that, by incurring expenditure which an ordinary prudent and uninsured owner would not have incurred, the insurers could not change a total loss into a partial loss.

Limitation of liability

The ordinary rules as to the award of civil damages for a wrong which has been done is that of compensation calculated to make good the actual loss suffered. A different principle, however, applies in admiralty matters, of which the yachtsman can take advantage, whereby ship owners who have caused loss by improper navigation are entitled to limit their liability. For the encouragement of shipping the 1894 Act and the Merchant Shipping (Liability of Shipowners and Others) Act 1958, in accordance with international conventions, confer a privilege of limitation of liability on ship owners measured by tonnage and expressed in gold francs as converted by sterling equivalent orders, later replaced by special drawing rights of the International Monetary Fund. As Lord Denning explained in the case of *Bramley Moore*: 'the principle underlying limitation of liability is that the wrongdoer should be liable according to the value of his ship and no more. A small ship has comparatively small value and it should have a correspondingly low measure of liability even though it is towing a great liner and does great damage. I agree there is not much room for justice in the rule but limitation of liability is not a matter of justice. It is a rule of public policy which has its origin in history and its justification in convenience.'

Section 17 of the Merchant Shipping Act 1979 now gives effect to the London Convention on the limitation of liability for marine claims of 1976. This raises the limits of liability, though they still remain favourable to the wrongdoer, and replaces the gold franc yardstick by units of account as defined by the IMF. The Act permits an owner to limit his liability in respect of loss of life or personal injury, or loss of or damage to property, but not if it is proved that the loss resulted from his personal act or omission committed with the intent to cause such loss, or recklessly and with knowledge that such loss would probably result. The ceiling limit in a claim for loss of life or personal injury is 333000 units of account for a ship with a tonnage not exceeding 500 tons, and 167000 units as to other claims. The units are a variable factor but for practical purposes an insurance cover of £500000 should constitute sufficient protection against the unexpected.

Third party risks

A marine policy may extend to claims made by third parties including passengers, but probably excluding members of the family and of crew and workmen on the boat for death, injury or damage occasioned by the insured yacht. The application of the statutory limitation of liability rule is a most relevant factor. In order to look after the situation where the ceiling limitation may not be applicable, an insurer may undertake to provide cover up to £500000 for third party indemnity including passenger liabilities. This can be reassuring to an owner, when it is recalled that £50000 was awarded to a man who fell out of a speedboat and was badly cut by the propeller; today those damages would be far higher.

Standard yacht policy

Under the terms of an average comprehensive policy provision may be made as to:

Cruising range
The cruising range may be stated to be by area, time, for a single voyage, or for a special cruise. The normal cruising limits offered may be:
  UK non-tidal.

10 mile radius of moorings.
UK Coastal and Inland.
UK-Dover/Calais/Brest/Scillies.
UK-Brest/Elbe.

Section 69 of the Customs and Excise Management Act 1979 and the Carriage of Goods Coastwise Regulations, give an indication as to those areas which may be regarded as coastal for the purpose of carrying goods between places in the United Kingdom; thus traffic between Liverpool and the Isle of Man is treated as coastwise. Inland waters include any part of the sea adjacent to the coast of the UK certified by the Secretary of State to be waters falling by international law to be treated as within the Queen's territorial sovereignty, apart from the operation of statute law in relation to territorial waters i.e. 3 nautical miles.

When planning a cruise a skipper should satisfy himself on his insurance cover as to area. It is easy to err. A snap decision at Honfleur to venture up the Seine may not appear to have been such a good idea when surveying the subsequent damage after a collision in fog at Caudebec. A skipper should therefore check that this situation is covered and, if in any doubt, should get written confirmation from his insurers in advance.

In commission/laid up

An owner must keep his eye on the calendar not only to ensure the renewal of his policy at the proper date, but also to appreciate if any limitations have been placed upon the time when the craft is deemed to be in commission and to arrange any desired extension. It follows that the longer the commissioned period the greater the premium. 'In commission' is the period when the yacht is fitted out, ready for sea, and available for the owner's immediate use. 'Laid up' is when the above state does not prevail and when the yacht is dismantled; generally the loose gear is stowed ashore, and the vessel during the period is kept as specified in the policy. During the laid up period the vessel must not be used for any purpose whatsoever other than dismantling, fitting out or customary overhauling, unless specifically mentioned in the policy (e.g. as living quarters).

Use

Use may be restricted in various ways such as limiting activities to private pleasure and cruising purposes only, and prohibiting any commercial or chartered employment of the craft. The towing of water skiers, or indeed of other craft, may be banned. A condition is normally imposed that the craft shall not be used as a houseboat. A vessel is said to be used as a houseboat when she is not used underway, or for navigation, but is kept on moorings, or at her berth, with the predominant object of living on board.

The insurance may be stated to be inapplicable to craft with a designed speed of over twelve knots, or to yachts when racing, unless special arrangement has been made. The policy may exclude employees of a ship yard, repair yard or slipway from using the vessel.

Loss/damage

Indemnity may apply to all loss of, or damage to, a craft caused by:

(1) external accidental means;
(2) stress of weather, stranding or collision;
(3) fire;
(4) theft of entire craft, or part, following *forcible entry*;
(5) governmental action in dealing with pollution hazard;
(6) sonic booms.

Normal cover does not extend to sails, or protective covers split by wind, or blown away whilst set, unless caused by the vessel grounding, or colliding while the sails are bent.

Repairs

The owner may be entitled to recover the cost of towing his vessel, if it is in distress, to a place of safety for any immediate necessary repairs. He may, however, be required to communicate in the manner prescribed under his policy with the underwriters, or their agents so as to get sanction for the estimated cost of the repairs to be done.

No claims

A no claims bonus clause often entitles an owner to an escalating percentage reduction over a period of years. It is not a 'no blame' clause and its interpretation is a matter within the discretion of the insurers; and this, if made in good faith, cannot be challenged. One method of protecting any loss of bonus is to get a written admission of liability or, better still, payment in full from the offending party.

Medical

Policies permitting of the recovery of medical charges vary; the scales of some tend to be on the low side. A prudent yachtsman should consider taking out separate medical cover to safeguard his family and crew against medical and dental expenses which may be incurred overseas outside the ambit of the National Health Service.

Legal

The insurers usually undertake liability for all legal charges properly incurred with their consent. This extends to any coroner's inquest, official inquiry or action in a court of law. In the event of a mishap the owner should:

(1) notify the underwriters, or their agents, in writing;
(2) give full information with details of all witnesses;
(3) make no admission as to liability;
(4) incur no legal expense without consent;
(5) forward all correspondence, unanswered, to the insurers;
(6) authorise the insurers to conduct all proceedings in his name;
(7) if the collision was in a race and a protest resulted, obtain a written copy of the protest committee's finding;
(8) if in foreign waters, contact the local agent.

It should be appreciated that notification under (1) and (8) must be made forthwith, or in any event within the time limit laid down in the policy, and failure to do so may result in avoidance of the claim.

Trailers

Before trailing any boat on the road, an owner should examine his motor insurance policy, and also the Motor Vehicles (Construction and Use) Regulations regarding the marking, maintenance and loading of trailers. The uninsured trailing of a boat on the public highway may lead to a fine, and even to loss of licence. An insurance policy may cover a trailer, provided it is maintained properly in accordance with the manufacturer's instructions, but not against fair wear and tear, or damage arising from immersion in salt water. Where a craft is not more than 7.62 metres (25 feet) in length, it may be covered whilst in transit, including the risks of loading and unloading but excluding scratching, bruising and denting. Where trailing or towing abroad, the foreign regulations should be consulted.

Check your insurance cover for trailing and racing risks

Safety requirements

In the absence of any legal requirements as to safety in small craft at sea, some insurers have made it a condition to recovery that certain safety precautions are observed. These are aimed to see that all care is displayed and that the craft is kept in a proper state of repair and seaworthiness. 'Seaworthiness' means that at the start of a voyage a ship shall be seaworthy for the purpose of

58

that particular venture, and reasonably fit in all respects to encounter the perils of the sea.

Gas installations

Gas containers and appliances are a notorious source of accidents as also of litigation. They have the potential of a floating bomb and should be treated with all respect. As a judge has said: 'The law expects of a man a great deal more care in carrying a pound of dynamite than a pound of butter. The law expects greater care if there is introduced on to an enclosed space in a ship a cylinder containing gas which may escape if precautions are not taken.'

Explosions and suffocation afloat often result from the misuse of bottled gas; hence insistence may be made that all tubing shall comply with the appropriate British Standard specification and that installation shall be inspected at regular intervals. An owner should be able to satisfy his insurers that he always checks for gas fumes before starting his engine, or striking a light below; he should also be able to show that, in the case of a gas refrigerator, there is proper ventilation.

Fuel

Reserve fuel should be carried to meet an emergency. An embargo is placed on stowing this in other than BS approved containers, as also in any part of a cabin.

Fire extinguishers

At least two up to date fire extinguishers properly charged and accessible must be maintained at all times.

Life jackets and safety harness

Terms of the policy may decree that life jackets are to be worn by non-swimmers in offshore tidal waters, and by the skipper and all aboard in winds of force four (sic) and over. More sophisticated policies may lay down conditions as to the use of safety harness (particularly at night) and the keeping of life rafts, life buoys and other safety equipment, stipulating the British Standard which is to apply.

Flares

Up to date distress signals should be carried at all times and kept in a dry and accessible place, the skipper and crew being aware of the emergency drill.

Radar

Craft when cruising may be required to hoist at an appropriate height an effective, correctly oriented, radar reflector at least four metres above sea level and unobstructed by sail.

Outboards

Outboards are especially vulnerable. It is not unusual for insurers to require that, if the outboard is left on the transom, it should be fastened to the boat by an approved locking device and not simply by the use of any padlock and chain. When not in use, the outboard should be kept in secure premises ashore. If, however, it is kept aboard, it should in any event be stowed in the cabin and locked up. Cover may be negotiated at an additional premium for dropping the outboard over the side. It is often a condition to compensation that the outboard be secured to the yacht or dinghy by an alternative method such as wire, chain or adequate line. The skipper should at all times have a note of the serial mark of the outboard and any other relevant details of identification.

Tenders

Cover may include tenders if an extra premium is paid. These must be properly and permanently marked with the name and home port of the parent craft, and be securely stowed when not in commission, and the serial number should be noted.

Racing risks

Racing risks are normally excluded unless special cover is obtained and for this charges can be high. Generally the comprehensive policy taken out by a family cruiser does not look after loss and/or damage to sails, masts, spars and rigging whilst she is racing. To get such protection, a Racing Extension Clause should be negotiated which will allow of full recovery for such loss or damage, calculated on the basis of the actual cost of replacement, and not of the current value ruling at the time when the policy was effected. A figure here to bear in mind is that an additional premium for such racing risks cover may be taken to be in the region of 2% of the declared cost of replacement.

Salvage charges

Salvage charges arise from the claim for a reward made by a person who saves, or assists in saving, a vessel or her cargo from jeopardy or capture; a comprehensive policy will clearly cover this. A tow for mere convenience does not come under this head.

Marinas

A marina may try to impose terms on a bertholder whereby he waives any rights of recovery that he might otherwise have against the marina. At the same time the operators of the marina may seek to retain a right to sue for loss or damage caused by the bertholder, his family or crew. All this means that the owner is discouraged from making any claim against the marina, but that the latter is free in certain circumstances to proceed against him. Thus any disputes falling into this category may have to be resolved between the respective insurers concerned.

Dinghies

Dinghy policies generally exclude cover for personal effects, as these are all too easily lost over the side. Another normal exclusion is made as to 'intentional self-injury, insanity, intemperance, suicide or attempted suicide; and the use of woodworking machinery or circular saws; as also persons under the age of 18 or over 70'.

Windsurfers

Board sailors must abide by the rules of the road and keep to the windy side of the law. They would do well to take out adequate cover for their equipment as also against third party claims for at least £500 000.

Illegality

Insurance does not embrace illegalities, for the courts will not enforce a contract which conflicts with public policy. Where undeclared jewellery was brought into the country and was later stolen, the court disallowed a claim under an All Risks policy. Smuggling goods into a friendly foreign country has the same disabling effect.

Arbitration

Arbitration is an alternative method for the resolution of differences either present or future by an arbitrator. It exists as an expeditious alternative to resorting to the regular courts of law and if the agreement is in writing it is governed by the Arbitration Acts 1950–79. Once an award has been made it may be enforced in the High Court. An insurance policy may contain an arbitration clause. Arbitration has the advantage that it is of an informal nature and is normally conducted in private. On the other hand the costs involved may perhaps be no less than, and may even exceed, the costs of an action, for the arbitrator's fees must be paid, usually by the losing party; a further point is that Legal Aid is not available for arbitration. In practice many disputes arising out of collision, and the majority of salvage claims, are referred to arbitration.

Renewal date

No days of grace are normally allowed on a marine insurance, so an owner must watch the calendar and see that his renewal premium is paid punctually. He should note that when a policy comes up for renewal both parties are free to make a new bargain.

Transfer

A policy of insurance is personal to the assured and cannot be transferred on the sale of a boat, which means that a buyer must arrange cover which is effective at the instant of the transfer.

Complaints

The Office of Fair Trading has encouraged the insurance industry to set up machinery for examining complaints by customers. Lloyd's have long had their own system of investigation and the British Insurance Association deals with matters relating to their members.

Cancellation

On the sale of a boat, an owner is entitled to the recovery of the unexpired portion of his premium. If, however, he is thinking of buying another boat in the near future he may ask that the policy be suspended on a *pro rata* basis against any future insurance required. If, on the other hand, he does not intend to buy another boat he may cancel the policy outright and obtain a refund of the balance of the premium paid which is calculated by the underwriters at short rate i.e. *pro rata* less 30%.

Check your cover

No one knows better than the sailor that nothing is more certain than that the uncertain is likely to happen. The optimist is said to be the man who lives with the pessimist, and the latter might take the view that although he may be insured against all conceivable combinations of calamities that the catastrophe which occurs is the very one against which he is not comprehensively covered. The average yachtsman can only assess the realistic risks involved in respect of which he can afford to invoke protection, and he should appreciate that there may be significant gaps in the cover contemplated on which he may well wish to have second thoughts. This is particularly relevant where transportation or craning of the craft is envisaged.

The need to insure the boat under construction against the possibility of the insolvency of the builder, and to see that indemnity is taken out at the appropriate stages of development, has already been stressed. At the point of delivery when a boat leaves the builder's yard the responsibility may shift from the builder to the buyer who should accordingly check his cover. It now depends on the policy effected as to whether there is adequate protection during the transit of the craft in the event of mishap. The contract may place responsibility on the transporter (whose own cover in this case should be inspected) but this ceases when the craft reaches its destination. Thereafter the boat may be craned, or trailed into the water, and this is certainly an occasion which calls for the reassurance that should this perchance miscarry compensation will be forthcoming. All these kind of matters should be investigated by an owner and discussed with his broker, for to be wise in time is nine tenths of wisdom, as was illustrated in the *Bab* Ballads:

'Down went the owners – greedy men whom hope of gain allured;
Oh, dry the starting tear, for they were heavily insured.'

4 Ashore, Afloat and Aground

The bowsprit got mixed with the rudder sometimes;
A thing, as the Bellman remarked,
That frequently happens in tropical climes,
When a vessel is, so to speak, 'snarked'.

Lewis Carroll
'The Hunting of the Snark'

Moorings

Once a craft has been acquired and insured the owner must decide where to keep it. The area chosen may affect his insurance premium, because underwriters know that, for the most part of her life, a yacht will be unattended and thus vulnerable to the moods of the weather and of vandals. A boat may be left ashore, in which case a licence to occupy space will depend on contract. It may be kept at moorings hired from a private owner, or public authority, in whom the land is vested on certain conditions. The Poole Harbour bye-laws, for instance, provide that no person shall place, lay down, maintain, use or have any mooring in the harbour without the licence of the Commissioners granted on stipulated terms. There is no right to put down permanent moorings in tidal waters where the bed is privately owned.

When granted, the licence bestows the right to the use of such mooring. By long custom among yachtsmen, a visitor seeing an unattended mooring may use it, but in terms of courtesy and of law, he must surrender it immediately to the true owner on the latter's return. The RYA has produced a useful docket which reads:

NOTICE TO VISITORS
Any person using this mooring in the
occupier's absence does so at his sole
risk and will be liable to pay harbour
dues. The owner and/or normal occupier
of this mooring reserves the right to

remove any vessel at the sole risk of
her owner.

This mooring has been used by a
sailing/motor vessel of ... metres LOA
... tons displacement.

An owner returning to his mooring and finding a stranger may
deal with him as a trespasser, which means in a reasonable way.
He may not cast him adrift; but he may shift him elsewhere. His
best course is to tie up alongside and either await the return of
the offender, or leave a note requiring him to depart. Any
precipitate damage done may disturb the insurers.

A 7 ton yacht in 1943 was on moorings belonging to the
Borough of Torquay, and became a casualty when her chain
parted in a gale. The judge, on a claim for damages, thought that
the mooring and swivel were sufficiently strong when laid in
1940, but had failed owing to rust and marine growth. The local
authority argued that they had not warranted the efficiency of
the chain. They had only undertaken to exercise reasonable care
and skill in selection and maintenance, and had relied on divers
who carried out an annual inspection. The local authority was
found liable, the judge holding that if moorings are only looked
at once a year, there ought to be a proper inspection, and that an
examination by a diver under water was inadequate, as it was
impossible for him to see small fractures or distortions of links
covered with mud, and that there had been 'a failure to carry out
the most important part of the examination nearest the spring
chain' (sic).

Plainly an owner should satisfy himself as to the strength of a
mooring, for if he ties up to an unsuitable one and does damage
he may have to pay. There is on record a notable event at Orford
when the distinguished skipper of the *Nona* picked up a buoy,
only to continue surging forward with it in full tow, to the
consternation of the local racing fleet, who had placed it there as
a turning mark. Doubtless they still tell the tale at the
Bembridge Sailing Club of the member whose boat parted from
moorings and was later recovered from the beach at Ostend
with the unfortunate result that he had to pay for an import
licence to retrieve her.

It has been held that the owner of a barge moored by a public footpath, where children were known to interfere, was liable for damages when it was cast adrift and collided with an eight-oared skiff.

Marinas

The term 'marina' is a comparative newcomer to the dictionary, and has come to denote a dock or basin with moorings for yachts and other small craft. The conditions are by no means uniform as between persons and places. Berths may be let or licensed on a long or short term basis. They may be within the disposition of a debenture holder, or assigned for some lesser term.

General regulations and conditions of berthing fixed by the National Yacht Harbour Association, and not necessarily agreed with or approved by the RYA, may obtain. The marina owner is at liberty to fix his own terms, and the remedy of an owner is to refuse them if he thinks they are unfair. It is early days to comment on the full legal implications of such terms, which do not so far seem to have been tested in any court of law. Although there can only be approval of those aimed at ensuring the comfort, safety and security of berth holders, concern has been expressed as to the opposition to sales and repairs from outside sources, and the annual escalation of mooring charges. An owner should read any proposed agreement with care and be aware of any special terms which may be imposed such as 'Where an owner arranges a private sale of a craft berthed, or usually berthed, in this Marina, he shall pay the Company 1% of the sale price as commission'.

Safety rules

Vessels of less than 13.7 metres (45 feet) in length are not subject to any specific statutory controls save that, by section 44 of the 1979 Act, if any person sends, or is party to sending a British ship to sea in such an unseaworthy state that the life of any person is likely to be endangered he is guilty of an offence. Furthermore if any person having command or charge of any ship knowingly takes the same to sea in such an unseaworthy state that the life of any person is likely to be endangered he commits an offence unless he can prove that her going to sea in such a state was in the circumstances reasonable and justifiable.

By section 428 of the 1894 Act it is the duty of an owner of every ship to see that his craft is provided with such appliances that are best adapted for securing the safety of all aboard in accordance with the rules set out as to the carrying of life saving appliances. These are prescribed by the Merchant Shipping (Life Saving Appliances) Rules 1965, along with which must be considered the Merchant Shipping (Fire Appliances) Rules 1965 as amended by regulations which lay down specific Department of Trade requirements applicable to pleasure craft over 13.7 metres (45 feet) in length.

Class XII pleasure craft, i.e. vessels of 13.7 to 21 metres (45 to 69 feet) LOA, if engaged on a voyage of more than three miles from the UK coast or a sea voyage from November to March, must have a liferaft, at least two efficient lifebuoys, a buoyant line, an approved lifejacket for each person aboard, a hand pump, six pyrotechnic distress signals, a spray nozzle, and two fire extinguishers.

As for small pleasure craft under 13.7 metres (45 feet) LOA, a working party invited by the government to consider the safety requirements of pleasure yachts which do not come under the statutory rules concluded that the widely differing usages to which they were put made regulations unsuitable for such vessels. They did, however, make certain recommendations for personal safety, rescue, fire fighting and general equipment intended as a guide to owners. These may be summarised as follows: Small craft of 5.5–13.7 metres in length should in any event be provided with adequate navigation lights and means of giving sound signals in order to comply with the Collision Regulations. A lifejacket and safety harness should be available for all on board as also at least two efficient lifebuoys with lights attached thereto. These should be backed up by flotation equipment such as a dinghy or inflatable liferaft. Fire fighting appliances and two buckets with lanyards should also be carried. In addition, all craft should have two anchors with appropriate warp or chain, bilge pump, compass, charts, six distress flares, first aid box, radio receiver, torch, radar reflector and engine tool kit. It may also be thought right to include a basic survival pack in case the ship has to be abandoned.

Although the recommendations do not have the force of law, failure to comply with them may tend to establish liability in any civil proceedings. Moreover an absence of appropriate appliances may affect any insurance claim which may arise; nor should it be overlooked that local regulations such as those prevailing on the River Thames may impose stringent safety requirements which do have the force of law.

In general the cruising yachtsman should study the memorandum on safety and the special regulations of the Royal Ocean Racing Club and aim to carry these into practice. On an owner's responsibility the RORC rightly say: 'The safety of a yacht and her crew is the sole and inescapable responsibility of the owner, who must do his best to ensure that the yacht is fully found, thoroughly seaworthy and manned by an experienced crew who are physically fit to face bad weather. He must be satisfied as to the soundness of hull, spars, rigging, sails and all gear. He must ensure that all safety equipment is properly maintained and stowed and that the crew know where it is kept and how it is to be used.'

Salvage

As Emerson reminds the yachtsman 'there are many advantages in sea voyages, but security is not one of them', thus if all safety precautions fail, the owner's mind may perforce turn to thoughts of salvage. As they say in Malta GC, even St Paul suffered shipwreck. When cruising in local waters the yachtsman is accustomed to the good natured help given by sailors known and unknown, who have no thought of reward as they themselves run aground in an effort to float a stranded yacht or, even if successful, manage to get the tow line wrapped round their own propeller. Often when such aid comes, the yachtsman has no time to weigh the legal niceties, or the logic, as to whether he should insist on passing his own line and ignore that flung by the rescuing vessel; still less does he consider debating over a loudhailer, or otherwise, whether the transaction be that of salvage or tow. Although strictly speaking the legal formalities, even in relation to a fellow yachtsman, should be observed, and inquiries made as to whether such services are to be rendered free or for value, an owner may rightly think that it would be unseemly to voice such a mundane question. In nine cases out of ten his assessment will be correct; if it is not, he must hope that the law will do what is right in the end. What is the law?

Salvage is the service rendered by a salvor, or a reward payable to him for his services. Such must be performed in rescuing life or property from danger on the water, and an owner must then pay a proper fee. Moreover the salvor has a right of lien, or detention, over the property for his services. Effective aid of any kind voluntarily given to a vessel or her cargo, in danger of loss or damage, may entitle those who render it to a salvage reward for such services as towing, piloting or navigation. Payment on the basis of salvage cannot be recovered where aid is only accepted on a towage footing.

The entitlement to salvage may derive from contract, but an actual agreement is not essential. Salvage is in essence a legal liability based on the rescue of property, whereby the owner upon whom benefit has been conferred shall reward his rescuer. It is a condition to the earning of remuneration that there has been danger to the ship salved at the material time. If there is no danger there can be no salvage. Salvage is rescuing a ship in peril and taking her to the nearest port of refuge. No agreement between parties can turn what is not a salvage into such a service.

Salvage then is the rendering of any voluntary help to a boat in real difficulties in tidal waters; it is an act giving rise to a right to claim a reward. Such reward is not payable to the crew of the endangered ship, nor to statutory officials carrying out public duties, such as a harbour master towing a vessel off a headland with his official launch.

The test as to whether a yacht is in fact in difficulties is a matter for the court; the burden of proof is on the salvors. Reward for salvage of life cannot be claimed as this is statutory duty; such a claim can only succeed if some part of the maritime property has been saved. Any award made is independent of contract, and a reasonable sum will be assessed, including all salvage expenses properly incurred. Once there has been a successful salvage, the salvors have a legal right of lien over the salved yacht and may detain her until their claim has been met. This includes a right to arrest and sell the ship and have her title vested in them.

Liens

A maritime lien is a right to detain a vessel as against payment for services rendered to her, and exists in the event of:

(1) Damage, or loss, caused by negligent navigation of a ship.
(2) Salvage.
(3) Expenses paid out by an owner.
(4) Bottomry i.e. pledging of the vessel, or cargo, to get money to complete the voyage.

Tow

There is an important distinction between salvage and tow. Tow is the product of negotiated agreement for the necessary use of means outside her own powers to aid a craft when she is not in

'Demonstrate that you are in command'

71

danger. An owner seeking a tow should demonstrate that he is in full command of his yacht, and he should agree the cost in advance, bearing in mind that a towing operation can sometimes turn into salvage and *vice versa*.

A yachtsman anxious about worsening conditions should decide whether it is imperative that he initiates a Mayday call. Once he makes any of the communications as set out in the Distress Signals Rules he will have triggered off the rescuing procedure for which he may be liable legally. Courts have held that the making of an emergency signal or the acceptance of help, may be evidence of the presence of danger. The legal lesson is to avoid making ambiguous signals as to danger.

Salvage services may be given by a boat answering a call for help, or by the mounting of an air-sea search. The RNLI, the Royal Navy and the RAF make no charge when saving life. The position as to property may be different and, in the case of HM Forces, by the Crown Proceedings Act 1947 they are at law in the same state as a private person.

Lifeboats

The Royal Lifeboat Institution is a charitable organisation incorporated by Royal Charter and supported entirely by voluntary subscriptions. It maintains lifeboats around the coasts dedicated to the saving of life from shipwreck. Lifeboat crews make no claim on a ship for life salvage. Their rules provide that no lifeboat may be used for salvage operations when tugs or other suitable craft are available and adequate. As for salvage of property the legal position was defined as long ago as 1904 in the case of the *Cargo Bonito*. Here it was said: 'If on arriving at the vessel in danger the services of the crew of the lifeboat are engaged in an endeavour to save the vessel, then as the crew become under the rules a party of salvors who have borrowed the lifeboat for property salvage purposes the launchers will be entitled to look to the owners of the property for salvage in respect of services rendered'. The onus is on the crew to show that they have given aid allowing them to be treated as property salvors.

In the *Viscount* in 1966, which was towed into port by the

Cromer lifeboat, after going aground in the fog on the Norfolk coast, a salvage claim by lifeboatmen was considered by the court. The *Viscount* said that a line had been passed after 200 duty free cigarettes had been tossed into the lifeboat. The court did not think that this was at all adequate and awarded £250. Again, where the Ramsgate lifeboat stood by a yacht which had lost its steering gear on Margate Sands, and gave her directions as to deeper water, a similar figure was recovered.

In the Fastnet Race disaster in 1979, the worst in yachting history, 15 lives were lost, 5 yachts were sunk and 19 abandoned but later recovered. A massive marine rescue operation was carried out by service helicopters, warships, merchant and fishing ships and lifeboats from both the UK and Eire. The RYA-RORC Report, chaired by Sir Hugh Forbes, recorded: 'in accordance with the traditions of the RNLI crewmen no salvage claims have been made in regard to these yachts.'

Truly the crews of the RNLI, along with the other rescuers, acted then as always in the heroic spirit of service at sea of which Winston Churchill, with his characteristic flair for paying fitting tribute to the brave, once spoke: 'It drives on with a mercy which does not quail in the presence of death. It drives on as a truth, a symbol, a testimony that man has been created in the image of God, and valour and virtue have not perished in the British race.'

Rescue services

The following acts of aid have been allowed by the courts as salvage: supplying a pump, fire extinguisher, anchor, warp or other tackle; furnishing a crew; standing by a vessel in distress, or giving directions as to local hazards over a loud hailer; operating as a communication centre to raise other assistance; separating vessels locked together, or preventing an impending collision; extinguishing a fire; pouring oil on the water; towing clear of danger.

It is difficult in an emergency for a skipper to keep a clear head and to reflect on the legal issues being raised, but he should show that he is in control of the situation by insisting on use of his own ropes, by not allowing rescuers to board his boat, and by being chary of accepting any anchor or gear. The message of this advice is simply to remind a skipper that it is as well to lay a viable basis which may induce a court to minimise any inflated claim which may be made. If gear is offered, and is all that is needed, then a sum should then and there be agreed.

No cure: no pay

Ideally the skipper should negotiate a written, or failing that an oral, agreement with the prospective salvors on the footing of tow. If this cannot be done, he should bargain along the lines of the simple form of salvage agreement recommended by the RYA in their publication *You and the Law*, written by Judge Andrew Phelan. This says that the contractor will use his best endeavours to salve the vessel and take her to a stated place, on the understanding of 'no cure: no pay', and that the contractor's fee if successful shall be £x or, failing that, such sum as may be awarded by an arbitrator to be appointed by the Secretary of Lloyd's.

Cost of salvage

Salvage is assessed on these principles:

(1) The value of the rescued yacht.
(2) The value of the rescued property.
(3) The risks to which they were exposed and the perils from which they were saved, including the possibility of any other assistance.
(4) The nature of the services rendered, including the skill displayed by the salvors and the time occupied in rendering the services.

The court will fix a sum which will fairly make good to the salvors what they have done, and such as will encourage them and others to keep similar equipment and give equal services as and when the need demands. Moreover an extortionate amount fixed *in terrorem* cannot be recovered, for the award will be assessed on the valuation of the yacht as salved and along reasonable lines of a *quantum meruit* (as much as the job was

74

worth). Thus where a yacht caught fire which was put out by the crew of a smack, they were awarded £750 as against the £3000 value of the yacht. The duty cast by the Merchant Shipping Acts and the Maritime Conventions Act to stand by and give aid does not shut out a claim for salvage.

HM Coastguard

If aid is given under contract, or in pursuance of an official duty, it is not a salvage service. HM Coastguard, for instance, have a responsibility for coordinating search and rescue operations around the 25000 miles of coastline of Great Britain and Northern Ireland. Founded in 1822 to put down smuggling, its modern role is one of complete dedication to the guarding and saving of life at sea. Full advantage should be taken of their Yacht and Boat Safety scheme. Help given outside the scope of the public duty of officials can be the subject of legal claim.

Harbour master

How stands the Harbour Master as to salvage and tow? In legal terms his position is governed by the Harbour Acts and the ordinary law. In practice a yacht in difficulties within the area of a harbour should seek aid from the Harbour Master and not from a local fisherman. Any award or bribe to such official is a criminal offence. In practice Harbour Masters, akin to HM Customs and Coastguards, are only too ready to help smooth the waters for yachtsmen. In strict terms of law a harbour authority can make a charge for services performed such as in giving a tow, but in practice this rarely occurs, and if it does, it may be expected to be on a reasonable basis, as opposed to the extortionate claims which some local fisherman may make. The authority is not precluded by any legislation in a clear case of salvage from pursuing a claim, but here again it may well be the policy of an authority not to press for this but merely to recover reasonable expenses. Accordingly a yachtsman in difficulty should wherever possible try to raise the Harbour Master, in preference to other seafarers, to his rescue.

The powers of this official derive from the harbour legislation

1847 to 1964 and from the bye–laws made thereunder. He gives directions regulating the ways of entry and exit from harbour, he approves the position of moorings, he gives permission for a yacht to lie in the entrance of the harbour, or at such place as he may order; he may remove any vessel anchoring without permission. The owner of a yacht may find himself liable for the expenses if he disobeys the reasonable instructions of a Harbour Master. Furthermore the Harbour Master is charged with the duty of keeping the harbour clear, and he has a right to remove unserviceable craft and offending obstructions and to charge for such service.

Marking wrecks

If a yacht sinks in the tideway of a navigable river, the owner is bound to take necessary precautions to stop danger to the public, and he cannot escape this liability by throwing the blame on any boatyard, or other contractor, employed by him to remove the craft. The rules were set out in the case of the *Snark*. She was wrecked in the tidal reaches of the Thames after a collision with a steamer. A boat flying a flag was fast, but this drifted away and a ship collided with the wreck. It was held that the owner was under a duty to give notice of the danger by lighting or buoying the place where the barge had sunk. Once this had been done his obligation was at an end, provided that the sinking had not arisen from his own fault. Furthermore an owner is under no duty to remove the wreck and if he abandons, or sells the ship, his liability ceases. A harbour or conservancy authority may remove a wreck in harbours or tidal waters if it is a danger to shipping, and they then resell it and satisfy all expenses out of the proceeds.

Pilotage and light dues

Pleasure craft and other small ships are so far exempt from compulsory pilotage under the Pilotage Act 1983. They also have the benefit of the facilities provided by lighthouses, buoys and beacons without payment. If over 20 tons they are liable, however, under the MS (Mercantile Marine Fund) Act 1898 to subscribe dues for these services.

Repairs

A mishap at sea will often lead to a yacht being taken for repair to a yard. If nothing is said at the time as to cost, the ordinary principles of law apply, which provide for such charges as would be thought reasonable between the parties, which are thus assessed on a *quantum meruit* basis (as much as the job is worth). This may have no relation to the yard's standard scale of charges. In practice business is frequently accepted by yards on the terms of a printed contract. The mere display of these terms in the office does not necessarily form an enforceable part of an agreement. If printed on the back of a form which the owner may sign, unless attention is directed overleaf, they are not part of the contract. Those relying on printed terms must specifically bring them to the attention of the owner and show that they have been accepted.

A yard has a particular lien on a ship for the cost of repairs. This means that when a debt has been incurred for labour or skill exercised upon a boat the creditor has an implied right of detention as against payment. *In extremis* a shipwrecked yachtsman may be compelled to carry out emergency repairs himself. G.K. Chesterton, when asked what book he would choose to have if marooned on a desert island, promptly replied: 'Brown's Practical Guide to Boatbuilding'.

5 Rules of the road

Both in safety, and in doubt,
Always keep a good look out.
In danger, with no room to turn,
Ease her, stop her, go astern.
                    Thomas Gray
            'Aids to Memory' 1877

Collision rules

The Collision Regulations and Distress Signals Order 1977 is an Order in Council giving legal force to the International Regulations for Preventing Collisions at Sea 1972. These replaced those of 1960 and now incorporate the modified traffic separation schemes, as also major changes in the steering and sailing rules, and in the requirements for navigation lights and hand signals. They are accepted by many countries including France, Germany, Greece, Netherlands, the USA and the USSR.

The Merchant Shipping (Distress Signals and Prevention of Collision) Regulations 1983 (No. 708) made under the Merchant Shipping Act 1979 adopt the Resolution of the Inter-Governmental Maritime Consultative Organisation. The Rules apply to all vessels upon the high seas and in all waters connected therewith navigable by seagoing vessels. They are written in the plain language of the sailor rather than of the lawyer. Each case arising under them depends in law on its merits. When the *Queen Mary* in World War II carved through her escorting cruiser *HMS Curacoa*, the court concluded that, as no special instructions had been given as to the navigation of ships in convoy, it was left to the master of each vessel to act as a seaman should. Nautical assessors may be invited to assist a court in maritime affairs. They may give an opinion on any matter relating to their expert cognisance, but the final decision is for the judge alone.

Having recited a rule, it may be rash to draw any binding

78

conclusions from cases which have come before the courts. The rules are issued for the guidance of sailors and must be read literally, but also construed with commonsense.

What was said by an American jurist would hold good here: 'Risk of collision begins the very moment when two vessels have approached so near each other, and upon such courses, that by a departure from the rules of navigation a collision might be brought about. It is true that *prima facie* each has the right to assume that the other will obey the law, but this does not justify shutting his eyes to what the other may actually do, or in omitting to do what he can to avoid an accident made imminent by the acts of the other.'

Keep a good look-out all round

It is a skipper's duty to see that all know the rules, and to impress on his crew that in the event of doubt, difficulty or danger he should be informed immediately.

The rules affect all vessels on the high seas, or in waters used by seagoing ships. They do not oust any local rules. 'Vessels' include every type of water craft; 'sailing vessel' means any vessel under sail provided that propelling machinery, if fitted, is not being used.

The underlying philosophy of the rules was once explained at a trial in this way: 'If you choose to drive a tandem across Salisbury Plain as fast as you like, and sway it from one side to the other, you are doing no harm to anybody else on Salisbury

79

Plain. But if there is somebody else on Salisbury Plain so near to you that by reason of your contiguity you are likely to run into him and damage him, then there arises a duty upon you not to be negligent, but to drive with reasonable care so as not to run into him. So it is with a ship at sea. She may go round and round in a circle and sail in any way she pleases if there is no other ship near her. But the moment there comes another ship, so near to her that if she navigates without due and reasonable regard for the other ship she may injure her, then the relative duties immediately arise. Besides those duties, which by universal custom determine what would be negligent steering or sailing, the Act of Parliament was passed which stated that when two sailing ships are approaching one another so as to involve risk of collision, then each of them is to do certain things. Those rules do really fix what under the circumstances will be negligent, unless those rules are broken by reason of inevitable accident.'

The rules do not in any way exonerate a skipper or crew from the consequences of the neglect of any precautions dictated by the ordinary practices of seamen, or by the special circumstances of the case. Conflict and inconsistency may make necessary a departure from the rules so as to avoid instant danger. Where a vessel is in breach of the rules, it is no defence to say that the breach was obvious because the courts have decreed that it is of the essence that the rules must be obeyed.

Statutory rules

The ordering of navigation up to the last century fell to the Trinity Brethren. Control was strengthened by Part V of the Merchant Shipping Act 1894. Section 418 (1) provides: 'Her Majesty may on the joint recommendation of the Admiralty and the Board of Trade by Order in Council make regulations for the prevention of collisions at sea, and may thereby regulate the lights to be carried and exhibited, the fog signals to be carried and used, and the steering and sailing rules to be observed by ships.'

Section 419 (1) says: 'All owners and masters of ships shall obey the Collision regulations and shall not carry or exhibit any

80

other lights, or use any other fog signals than such as are required by those regulations.'

Section 419 (2) states that if an infringement is caused by the wilful default of the master or owner of a ship he shall be guilty of a criminal offence. Section 419 (3) allows for a defence if it is shown to the satisfaction of the court that the circumstances of the case make a departure from the regulations necessary.

By section 680 any offence under the Act is punishable by a fine, or imprisonment with or without hard labour. It may perhaps be some small consolation to know that hard labour has since been abolished! If an offender is tried by the magistrates there is a ceiling penalty of 6 months imprisonment and/or a fine. A recent case in the courts establishes that a defendant appearing before the Justices on an information charging him with an offence under section 419 is entitled to elect to be tried by them or by a jury.

Court rulings

From the findings of the magistrates there is a right of appeal by the defendant and also on a matter of law by the prosecutor. One such appeal arose where a master of a ship had handed over the wheel to his mate who had then collided with a bridge. Both were prosecuted under section 108 (a) of the Port of London Act 1969 for having navigated without due care and attention. The Justices dismissed the case. The prosecutor appealed. The Divisional Court allowed the appeal saying that 'to navigate' was not restricted to actually steering the vessel, and that the true master was navigating the ship in the sense that he was directing its course and was responsible for it on the river.

In another recent case the master of a vessel was alleged to have infringed a traffic separation scheme in breach of R. 10(d) of the 1977 Regulations. His defence, which the magistrates accepted, was that he was not in wilful default as he did not consider his ship to be through traffic and was hence right to use the inshore zone. The prosecutor appealed to the Divisional Court who held that the master's belief did not make his act innocent for ignorance of a statutory provision was no defence.

On the other hand in *Bradshaw* v. *Ewart James* 1983 1 All ER

12, the master of a ship in the English Channel handed over the wheel to his chief officer with the orders to steer a course which, with the tide, would comply with Rule 10 (c). The ship was sailed on a contrary course. The master was charged that, in crossing traffic lanes, he had failed to cross as nearly as practicable at right angles to the general flow of traffic in breach of sections 419 and 680 of the 1894 Act and Rule 10 (c) of the 1972 Rules. The Justices dismissed the case on the grounds that the master had no knowledge of the offence and was not deliberately negligent. The Secretary of State for Trade appealed to the Divisional Court arguing that section 419 (1) imposed an absolute obligation. The Lord Chief Justice, whilst allowing that this did fix an absolute civil obligation, found that it did not constitute an absolute criminal offence and that there was here no *mens rea*. He accordingly dismissed the appeal.

Maritime Conventions Act 1911

It is for a court to apportion liability under the Maritime Conventions Act 1911, where damage is caused, in proportion to the degree which each vessel is to blame. Where the parties are equally to blame, or where it is impossible to distinguish the comparative degrees of responsibility, liability is assigned equally. Where, by the fault of two or more vessels, damage or loss is caused to one or more of those vessels, the liability to make good the damage or loss shall be in proportion to the degree in which each vessel was at fault. Questions of causation are apportioned by the law in a broad commonsense way, and not by reference to scientific or philosophic theories.

Sailing and steering rules

Look out and safe speed

The steering and sailing rules deal with the conduct of vessels in any condition of visibility. They impose a duty on every vessel to maintain at all times a proper look out, by sight and hearing, by all available means appropriate in the prevailing circumstances and conditions, so as to make a full appraisal of the situation. Every vessel shall at all times proceed at a safe speed, so that she can take proper and effective action to avoid collision, or be stopped within a distance suitable to the current conditions, after taking into account such matters as the state of visibility, traffic density, stopping distance and the state of the wind, sea and tide.

To establish liability for a collision on the part of a ship, it is not sufficient merely to show that she had a bad look-out; it must be shown that the bad look-out contributed to the collision and to the damage. This in no way detracts from the admirable advice given in the *Seaway Code*: above all keep a good look out all round.

Giving way

Section 11 of the IRPCS applies to the conduct of vessels in sight of one another and deals with the drill of giving way by a sailing vessel, overtaking, and a head-on situation under engine. All who take the helm should be familiar with these rules and those such as children who may be allowed to take the tiller should, if not so schooled, be supervised. Rule 12 provides that when two sailing vessels are approaching one another so as to involve risk of collision, one of them shall keep out of the way of the other, as follows:

(1) when each has the wind on a different side, the vessel which has the wind on the port side shall keep out of the way of the other;
(2) when both have the wind on the same side, the vessel which is to windward shall keep out of the way of the vessel which is to leeward;
(3) if a vessel with the wind on the port side sees a vessel to windward and cannot determine with certainty whether the vessel has the wind on the port or on the starboard side, she shall keep out of the way of the other.

Rule 13 expresses ordinary sea sense in placing the onus on an overtaking boat to keep clear. Rule 14 says that when two power-driven vessels are meeting on reciprocal or nearly reciprocal courses so as to involve risk of collision each shall alter her course to starboard so that each shall pass on the port side of the other.

Narrow channels

By Rule 9, a vessel of less than 20 metres, or a sailing vessel, shall not impede the passage of a vessel which can safely navigate only within a narrow channel or fairway; a vessel proceeding along such a channel shall be as near to the outer limit which lies on her starboard side as is safe and practicable. A court ruling on what is regarded to be mid-channel denotes it as the centre line of the dredged channel, and not the centre of the navigable water as a whole. In the case of the *Knaresboro* it was said that a vessel going out of, or coming into, a narrow harbour entrance ought not to cross the entrance so close as not to leave room for vessels going the other way, but ought to make a wide sweep so as to leave them a fairway. In narrow channels, regard should be paid to the manoeuvres which other craft may have to take in avoiding larger vessels. Any vessel shall avoid anchoring in a narrow channel.

All the cases show that the yachtsman should be alive to the problems of large vessels, barges towed by tugs, passenger service vessels and other commercial traffic. A vessel crossing a channel has no right of way over a vessel proceeding up and down, and must give way. At all times a careful look out should be kept astern as also ahead.

Traffic separation schemes

Traffic separation schemes are set out in Admiralty Notices to Mariners published by the Hydrographer of the Navy. They are marked on Admiralty charts, and digested in nautical almanacs. They denote areas of high concentration of shipping and have been established in the interests of safety. It is an offence for any British ship using any traffic separation scheme to proceed against the regular direction of traffic flow.

Rule 10 reads:

(a) This Rule applies to traffic separation schemes adopted by the Organization:

(b) A vessel using a traffic separation scheme shall:

(1) proceed in the appropriate traffic lane in the general direction of traffic flow for that lane;

(2) so far as practicable keep clear of a traffic separation line or separation zone;

(3) normally join or leave a traffic lane at the termination of the lane, but when joining or leaving from the side shall do so at as small an angle to the general direction of traffic flow, as practicable.

(c) *A vessel shall so far as practicable avoid crossing traffic lanes, but if obliged to do so shall cross as nearly as practicable at right angles to the general direction of traffic flow.*

(d) Inshore traffic zones shall not normally be used by through traffic which can safely use the appropriate traffic lane within the adjacent traffic separation scheme. *However vessels of less than 20 metres in length and sailing vessels may under all circumstances use inshore traffic zones.*

(e) A vessel, other than a crossing or joining vessel, shall not normally enter a separation zone or cross a separation line except:

(1) in cases of emergency to avoid immediate danger;

(2) to engage in fishing within a separation zone.

(f) A vessel navigating in areas near the terminations of traffic separation schemes shall do so with particular caution.

(g) A vessel shall so far as practicable avoid anchoring in a traffic separation scheme or in areas near its terminations.

(h) A vessel not using a traffic separation scheme shall avoid it by as wide a margin as is practicable.

(i) A vessel engaged in fishing shall not impede the passage of any vessel following a traffic lane.

(j) A vessel of less than 20 metres in length or a sailing vessel shall not impede the safe passage of a power-driven vessel following a traffic lane.

Merchant Shipping Notice No. 645 informs owners of yachts that the Department of Trade consider it important that any vessel observed in a traffic separation scheme which appears to be navigating otherwise than in accordance with the established principles of such schemes is advised of the fact at the time by means of a special signal which is that of the letters YG meaning: 'You appear to be contravening the rules of a traffic separation scheme'. An owner on receiving the signal by whatever means should take immediate action to check his course and position and take any further steps which appear to him appropriate in the circumstances.

Infringement of Rule 10 is a criminal offence which renders the offender liable to prosecution in the magistrates' court and on conviction to a fine.

Rule 10 is not without its difficulties. It is couched in mandatory terms to the effect that if a traffic lane is to be crossed, it should be done as nearly as practicable at right angles. In order to comply with this requirement it may mean that a yacht will have to use her engine (if any). There has been seamanlike controversy as to what is meant by a 90 degree crossing of a traffic lane. One view expressed is that it is a 90 degree track across the lane; another that it is a 90 degree angle of heading. So far such decisions in relation to yachts that have been given have been by lay justices, in the face of strong representations by the Department of Trade, and until there is a change in the Regulations or an authoritative ruling by the Divisional Court on appeal there may, in the absence of any firm case law, be differences of opinion on interpretation. However the generally accepted understanding of the requirement among a body of seamen, and sea lawyers alike, is that a yacht should steer at right angles to the oncoming traffic flow, even though tracking with leeway, rather than make good a course at right angles but steering obliquely to allow for leeway and tide effect. Thus it would seem that it is the heading rather than the track that applies and that this should be as nearly as practicable at right angles to the direction of the traffic flow.

The object of the rule must be taken to require yachts to demonstrate a clear and decisive intent which can be readily understood, and so remove any misunderstandings or miscalculations in the mind of the officer on watch on the bridge of big ships, whose stopping and manoeuvring abilities may be extremely restricted. Bearing in mind the grave consequences which can stem from any infringement of the Anti-Collision Regulations, it is perhaps not surprising that magistrates appear to be applying the same stringent tests as to culpability, and severity of pecuniary penalty, that they have been constantly counselled by successive Lord Chancellors to impose in the interests of road safety, and the preservation of life, in their enforcement of the road traffic legislation, particularly as it relates to the motorways.

Radar scanners monitor the Dover Straits and have been responsible for detecting rogue yachts contravening the rules. There is a discretion on the part of the Department of Trade whether to prosecute or not. Any allegation of breach is analysed in the first instance by the Marine Surveyor of the Department of Trade and thereafter, if satisfied after examining the evidence, including any oral or written statement from the alleged offender, that there has been a blatant disregard amounting to an unwillingness to comply with the regulations, it is reported to their solicitors to consider taking process in the criminal courts. The decision to prosecute offenders rests finally with the Department of Trade, who have in a press release warned yachtsmen that action will be taken for any flagrant breach of the rules, switching traffic lanes, sailing against the general flow of shipping, and cutting across the path of other vessels. They assert that the policy of the Department is to adopt a flexible approach to the regulations, taking into account the problems facing yachts under sail, and exercising their discretion not to prosecute in appropriate cases.

Lights

Under Rules 20–31 lights must be exhibited from sunset to sunrise and in restricted visibility. The incident of *HMS Truculent* illustrates the task of interpretation with which the navigator may be faced. This submarine collided with the tanker *Divina* during the hours of darkness with a tragic loss of life. As she was carrying a flammable cargo, the *Divina* had a red light at her masthead which was misread by *HMS Truculent* to be that of a moored vessel stationary in the channel. The lights on *HMS Truculent* were insufficient and gave the misleading impression that she was an extremely small vessel. It was accepted by the parties that the liability of the Admiralty for the collision was that of 75%, and that the *Divina* was 25% to blame.

Sailing vessels under way and vessels under oars

Rule 25 provides as follows:

(a) A sailing vessel under way shall exhibit:
   (1) sidelights;
   (2) a stern light.

(b) In a sailing vessel less than 20 metres long, these lights may be combined in one lantern carried at or near the top of the mast where it can best be seen.

(c) A sailing vessel under way may, in addition to the lights at (a) above, exhibit at or near the top of the mast, where they can best be seen, two all round lights in a vertical line, the upper being red and the lower green but these shall not be exhibited in conjunction with the combined lantern permitted by (b).

(d)
   (1) A sailing vessel of less than 7 metres long shall if practicable exhibit the lights at (a) or (b), but if she does not she shall have ready at hand an electric torch or lighted lantern showing a white light, which shall be exhibited in sufficient time to prevent collision.
   (2) A vessel under oars may exhibit the lights prescribed in this Rule for sailing vessels, but if she does not, she shall have ready at hand an electric torch, or lighted lantern, showing a white light which shall be exhibited in sufficient time to prevent collision.

(e) A vessel proceeding under sail, when also being propelled by machinery, shall by day exhibit forward where it can best be seen a conical shape, apex downwards.

It is to be noted that there is a legal requirement under the Collision Rules that all vessels must be equipped with adequate navigation lights and have the means of giving efficient sound signals at sea.

Anchored

A vessel at anchor shall exhibit where they can best be seen certain specified lights; this requirement does not stop her from using lights to illuminate her decks as indeed big boats are required to do. A vessel of less than 50 metres in length may exhibit an all-round white light where it can best be seen. A vessel of less than 7 metres in length, when at anchor and not in or near a narrow channel, fairway or anchorage, or where other vessels normally navigate shall not be required to exhibit lights or shapes. An anchor light should not be displayed at the time when a yacht is slipping her mooring to get under way. Hence in the *Ialine* it was ruled that a vessel was justified in crossing close to the bows of *Ialine* which was, in fact, moving ahead, although showing the all round white 'at anchor' light. Being at anchor is a nautical phrase which everybody understands. It is not necessary that an anchor should be down, for instance a vessel made fast to a mooring has no anchor of her own, and fishing boats have been brought up by casting a heavy stone overboard with a line attached.

The lights of fishing vessels sometimes seem to suggest that they have a private law of their own. In a recent case it was said that, even though it may be general practice for fishing vessels at anchor at certain localities not to exhibit anchor lights, yet they may be at fault in not showing them.

Any light to attract the attention of another vessel must be such that it cannot be mistaken for any aid to navigation; the use of intermittent or revolving lights, such as strobe lights must be avoided.

River Thames

The tidal Thames comes under the Port of London Authority and extends for 93 miles from Margate Sand to Teddington Lock. There are no specific byelaws as to the navigation of private craft; such craft must comply with the Port of London River Byelaws made under the Port of London Act which are primarily intended for the regulation of commercial vessels. Any offence against the byelaws, as also the international rules of the road which are incorporated, carries a fine. Above Wandsworth there is a speed limit of 8 knots; there is no legal limit below, but excessive speed liable to cause damage to persons or property may attract a heavy fine.

The byelaws add to the sound and other signals which normally apply, and remind the yachtsman that commercial craft have difficulties in manoeuvring, as do tugs towing barges, and vessels whose draught confines them to the deep water channel. The Act provides. 'If the life of any person, or the safety of any vessel, mooring, bank or other property is endangered, or injury or damage is caused to any person, vessel, mooring, bank or other property by a passing vessel, the onus shall lie upon the master of such passing vessel to show that she was navigated with care and caution and at such a speed and in such a manner as directed.'

The upper, non-tidal Thames stretches for 135 miles from Teddington Lock to Cricklade in Wiltshire, coming under the Thames Water Authority, and is controlled by the Thames Conservancy Acts, Orders and Byelaws 1932–1974. These require all pleasure craft, including tenders and inflatables, to be registered and licensed. Navigation lights must be exhibited when navigating between sunset and sunrise, and the requirements are not met by tricolour or bicolour lights. Every launch must be fitted with a whistle or horn; speed is restricted to 7 knots, and all steps must be taken to ensure that wash will not menace children, punts or canoes. There have been many instances when, through the carelessness of passing craft, crockery has been broken and scalding liquids upset. It is an offence punishable with a fine to navigate without due care and caution, or to endanger other persons, boats or banks. Two convictions for careless or improper navigation led to automatic loss of registration. No sewage and other polluting wastes may be deposited in the river; the only sanitary appliances approved are the chemical and recirculation types that do not discharge overboard.

Sailing craft need to keep a special eye open for fishermen on banks who are not without their rights. As the Thames River Users' Code has it: 'manners makeyth man'. It seems that one arch law-maker, Disraeli, lapsed somewhat from this standard when he said of his opponent Gladstone: 'If he fell into the Thames it would be a misfortune, but if someone dragged him out it would be a calamity.'

Rule in the Bywell Castle

The most tragic disaster ever to be recorded on the Thames happened at 1930 hours on the 3rd September 1878 when 640 day-trippers aboard the paddle steamer the *Princess Alice* lost their lives at Galleon's Reach off Woolwich. A collier, the *Bywell Castle*, was proceeding downstream on a parallel course of red to red. But suddenly the *Princess Alice* put her helm hard to port. The *Bywell Castle*, now seeing a green light, ported into it. She could not have made a worse manoeuvre. The paddle steamer was struck and sunk. The Court of Appeal found that she alone was to blame. She had been navigated in a careless and reckless manner paying no regard to speed and look out. The Thames Yacht Club protested that yachtsmen were bewildered by the extraordinary way in which steamships behaved. The rules of the river were thereafter changed and strengthened. What emerged from the ruling of the court is of general application to emergency situations both on land and at sea. Though the *Bywell Castle* had herself made an erroneous response she was exonerated from legal blame. She had reacted in the agony of the moment as one might do who, through the fault of another, had lost her nerve. The court said: 'A ship has no right by its own misconduct to put another ship into a situation of extreme peril and then charge the other ship with misconduct. There was no right to expect men to be something more than ordinary men. In this situation the same amount of skill is not to be expected as under ordinary circumstances.'

Recording collisions

If a collision causes damage to a vessel, personal injury or loss of life, a full note should be made immediately or at the earliest opportunity whilst the incident is fresh in mind. It should be recorded preferably in the ship's log and be signed by the skipper and any witnesses. Such an entry will be of help not only in any insurance claim, but may be relied on in any subsequent court or arbitration proceedings to refresh memory and add to the weight of evidence.

In any event, rules of the court lay down that in a collision claim certain information must be given. Thus it is that any note made should include:

(1) the names and registered ports of the relevant ships;
(2) the date, time and place of collision;
(3) weather, wind, tidal conditions;
(4) course and speed;
(5) lights (if any) carried by the ships;
(6) sound signals (if any) given;
(7) the parts of each ship which came into collision.

Other matters such as any relevant signals seen, or words heard before, at, or after the collision should be mentioned. A diagram of the position immediately before and at the time of impact will also help; so too (if very fortunate) a counter-signature in the log by the master of the other vessel. An owner should also be ready to produce a chart marked with the yacht's position. Photographs taken at the time may assist.

Reporting

If there has been a loss of life, serious personal injury, or damage affecting seaworthiness or efficiency, as a result of an impact at sea, then a written report must be made under the 1894 Act as soon as possible to the Department of Trade and Industry.

Log

The average yachtsman is not under any legal compulsion to keep a log, though of course it is a matter of good seamanlike practice so to do. One of the advantages of keeping one is that an entry may be admissible in evidence in a civil or criminal trial. To what extent entries will be admissible is for a court to say. The layman may still find the problem as baffling as did Sam Weller. 'Little to do and plenty to get I suppose?' asked Sergeant Buzfuz jocularly. 'Oh, quite enough to get, Sir, as the soldier said when they ordered him 350 lashes', replied Sam. This, it will be recalled, brought that deathless rebuke from the

92

judge, 'You must not tell us what the soldier or any other man has said, Sir, it's not evidence'.

The rules of evidence and other legal rules may appear to be pure Greek not only to Sam Weller, but to other natives of these shores. Lord Darling once remarked 'I am afraid I never learned Greek and know nothing of their language. All I remember reading about the Greeks was that they sent out a number of ships, the majority of which were wrecked. As far as I can understand from reading the Law Reports, they have been doing the same thing ever since.'

In general for the better avoidance of disaster at sea the caution given by Rule 2 of the Collision Regulations should never be far from mind: 'due regard shall be had to all dangers of navigation and collision and to any special circumstances which make a departure from the Rules necessary to avoid immediate danger.' An old salt will never allow slavish scientific adherence to specific rules to outplay common sea sense. Not for him the epitaph writ in water of one luckless mariner:

Here lies the body of Michael O'Day
Who died maintaining his right of way.
He was right, dead right, as he sailed along
But he's just as dead as if he'd been wrong.

6 Venturing Overseas

'What matters it how far we go?' his scaly friend
  replied,
'There is another shore, you know, upon the other side,
The further off from England, the nearer is to France –
Then turn not pale, beloved snail, but come and join
  the dance'.

Lewis Carroll
'Alice's Adventures in Wonderland.'

Documents

A yachtsman planning to cruise overseas must give thought to
the legal formalities involved. He should see that the ship's
papers are in order; these may include any documents relative to
the ownership or chartering of the craft, as also his insurance
policy. Prior to sailing, although under no legal compulsion, he
should as a safety measure notify the Coastguard of his
proposed movements.

A skipper and his crew should check that they have with them
valid passports with any necessary visas. Such passports should
be carried when ashore abroad, and a separate note kept of their
number and date and place of issue. A passport is the property
of HM Government and cannot be used as a security for a
private debt; in the event of loss the Police should be notified, as
also a British Consul for the issue of a duplicate. Consular
officers are there to help British subjects overseas in cases of
need. The telegraphic address of all British Consulates is that of
'Britain' followed by the name of the town.

The procedure to be followed by yachts going foreign is set
out in HM Customs and Excise Notices. Yachts, like any other
British ships, are subject to Customs control when going foreign
or returning from such parts (which include Eire and the
Channel Islands); the test of a yacht is private ownership and
user. As a concession to those using their boats for purely
pleasure purposes, the Commissioners permit certain relax-
ations.

To satisfy continental requirements an owner needs a
certificate of registry under Part 1 of the 1894 Act, or a small

ship's certificate issued by the RYA under the 1983 Regulations. If the boat is on loan or charter, he should see that this is properly documented and that the VAT status of the vessel can be established. He will as a matter of good sea sense have proper charts and up to date hydrographic information. Indeed this is mandatory in the case of craft of 12 metres or over, by the 1975 Rules.

Colours

The skipper must also have aboard the proper national colours namely either the red or an entitled privileged Ensign and the yellow international code flag Q (my vessel is healthy and I request free pratique). Failure to fly a Q flag on returning to UK territorial waters can lead to a fine of up to £200. He might also think it right to include distress signal flags (NC) and courtesy flags of the countries to be visited, taking care not to confuse the French colours with the Dutch! He will of course, if going further than the Channel Islands or Eire, have put any pets into kennels or other form of care. Those tempted to the contrary should be well aware of the criminal folly in trying to cheat the protective anti-rabies legislation.

Insurance

Insurance against boating risks is not compulsory in the UK but it can be in certain foreign countries. In any event an owner should be comprehensively covered for the waters in which he is likely to cruise, extended if need be to inland rivers and canals. If his policy does not include medical and dental treatment overseas he should remind himself that this can be very expensive and that it may be prudent to arrange separate travel insurance to meet the contingent charges. He may also take the precaution of contacting his local DHSS office, after noting his NHS number, and those of the family, asking for leaflet SA 30 on medical costs abroad, and requesting Form 111, a Certificate of Entitlement which permits him as part of reciprocal agreements to take advantage of medical services available to EEC nationals and to recover his costs on his return at approximately three-quarters of any amount which he may have paid.

Notice of departure

Those going foreign should get from HM Customs and Excise the current booklet: *Notice to Owners and Persons Responsible for Pleasure Craft Based in the United Kingdom* (N.8). This, with the forms C 1328, i.e. Notice of Intended Departure and Report of Arrival Declaration, are obtainable free of charge from most Customs offices and some yacht clubs. The forms need to be completed with great care as there are heavy penalties for making false declarations.

By section 81 of the Customs and Excise Management Act 1979, a small ship means a ship not exceeding 100 tons in respect of which the Commissioners may make general regulations. Under the Act the Pleasure Craft (Arrival and Report) Regulations 1979 have been made with which the skipper of any vessel going foreign, which includes the Channel Islands and the Republic of Eire but not the Isle of Man or any part of the United Kingdom, should be familiar. The Regulations say that a pleasure craft means:

(a) a vessel being used for private recreational purposes and of which the total complement including passengers and crew does not exceed 12 persons; or

(b) any other vessel which a Customs officer agrees to treat as such.

It is part of the freedom of the seas which a yachtsman under the law of England enjoys that he can depart from and arrive at any place in the UK. At the same time there are certain demands that the law makes and these include the giving of written notice of departure and arrival. The Notice of Intended Departure form must be completed by the responsible person in command. This requires particulars of the name of the vessel, registration number, description, colour, length in metres and tonnage; place where built and normally moored or berthed. A declaration must be made as to whether the ship is on hire, charter or loan and as to whether VAT has been paid on it or its equipment. The place and time of departure, destination and expected date and place of return must be entered along with details of any animals or birds. The names, passport numbers, dates of birth and nationality of all on board must be supplied. Failure to give prior notice may result in prosecution and a fine of £200. The notice is valid for 48 hours after the stated time of departure. In the event of the voyage being abandoned the forms must be returned to the Customs with an endorsement to that effect. If HM Coastguard have been alerted under the Yacht Boat Safety Scheme, they should also be notified.

Foreign arrival

On entering a foreign port the national colours and the Q flag should be hoisted to which may be added the appropriate courtesy flag. The skipper will comply with and clear the local formalities. In doing all this he may be assisted by including in his ship's library the RYA publication *Planning for Going Foreign*. In the case of a visit to France an approach to the French Government Tourist Office requesting their yachting literature setting out the legal requirements may be helpful. The yachtsman must abide by the laws of the land which he visits, at the same time remembering that though far from the shores of England he may still be liable to the jurisdiction of its criminal and civil courts.

A skipper should make a note of all goods he buys to take home for the burden of proof as to whether duty has been paid or not rests with the importer. He should particularly keep all receipts as to any items of marine equipment purchased, i.e. of any repairs, alterations or additions carried out to the boat or her engine, as these may be liable to duty including VAT. If he runs into financial difficulties arising out of an emergency, such as extensive boat repairs or hospital charges to which his travellers' cheques or Euro credit card do not extend, he may perhaps be minded to contact the nearest British Consulate in the hope that a loan may be arranged.

Return

On the return voyage the skipper should fly his ensign and a Q flag which if it be dark should be suitably illuminated (probably more easily said than done!). On arrival he should notify a Customs Officer either in person or by freephone telephone. This must be done within two hours of arrival, save if this is between 2300 and 0600 hours notification need not be made until 0800 hours.

Quick report

If the boat is not boarded within two hours of reporting arrival the complement may take advantage of the Quick Report procedure if there is nothing to declare and, provided all the requirements set out in the advisory booklet Notice 8 are satisfied, they can cross so to speak through the green sector. The Report of Arrival from Foreign must however have been completed and deposited in a Customs or Post Office box. This form requires *inter alia* particulars of time and place of arrival, last port of call and details of any duty-free stores, repairs and additions. A full account must be given of all stores and goods liable to customs duty and/or VAT and in particular of tobacco, spirits, firearms and medicinal drugs. All persons on board must sign the declaration relating to personal goods.

Full report

Advantage cannot be taken of the Quick Report procedure if there is anything to declare, nor if the matters set out in Notice 8 obtain, such as the lack of a valid British passport, or if there has been a death or notifiable illness on board. In this case the skipper must complete the Arrival Report and have it ready for the Customs officer when he calls. Meanwhile no one should be allowed aboard until formal clearance. When the officer visits, the skipper will hand over the form and answer all such questions as may be put, paying such duty and/or VAT as may be due. Everything got abroad must be declared. After satisfying the health, customs and immigration requirements, the master will be handed a certificate of 'free pratique' under the Public Health (Ships) Regulations and now hauls down the yellow flag. Failure to comply with the report requirements may lead to a fine of £200. Between 1981 and 1983 over 750 oral and written warnings were given to defaulting yachtsmen. Reliance cannot necessarily be placed on such indulgence and it is to be observed that there have been a number of successful and notable prosecutions in the magistrates' courts.

Stores

In general no restrictions are imposed upon the shipment of reasonable quantities of food and fuel, but duty-free stores are normally restricted to vessels over 40 tons, and in any event formal outward clearance is needed when duty-free stores are shipped. Allowance may be made for taking aboard duty-free stores on craft proceeding outside home trade limits i.e. south of Brest, or north of the north bank of the Elbe. Such stores must be placed under Customs' seal on board, and may not be used in home waters without payment of duty and VAT. Foreign going ships may ask for certain goods which are subject to VAT to be zero rated, if the formalities are observed and the goods are delivered direct to the vessel. Information as to the shipment of bonded stores may be got from approved merchants at the main ports. No goods other than *bona fide* stores and personal effects may be shipped unless all relevant export licensing and other formalities are met.

Immigration

All persons not having the right of abode in the UK need the permission of an immigration officer to embark when foreign bound, and the owner is responsible for seeing that this is done.

Drugs

The Misuse of Drugs Act 1971 prohibits the production, importation, exportation, possession and supply of controlled drugs unless properly authorised, as for instance by prescription of a doctor, or by permission of the Home Office. The Act allows the owner of a ship which does not carry a doctor to have specialised drugs for the purpose of compliance with the Merchant Shipping Acts.

One of the main objects of HM Customs is to prevent the introduction of dangerous drugs into the country. Trafficking in these is a world-wide and expanding problem. The Lord Chief Justice, Lord Lane, in laying down the sentencing guidelines for offences under the Misuse of Drugs Act 1971 has commented that one of the most terrifying aspects which comes with hard drugs is the degradation and suffering and, not infrequently, the death of the addict adding: 'It is not difficult to understand why in some parts of the world traffickers in heroin in any substantial quantity are sentenced to death and executed.'

The 1971 Act divides dangerous drugs into three classes A, B and C according to their potency. In assessing the culpability of an offender a distinction is made between those who are in possession of the prohibited substance with the intention of supply for profit, and those who possess purely for their own personal consumption. Smuggling drugs into the UK contrary to the 1971 Act is an aggravating feature. Parliament has provided that penalties may range from a fine to life imprisonment.

The tariff for importing Class A heroin and morphine to the street value of £100000 is that of 7 years and upwards. For simple possession for personal consumption there are many cases where deprivation of liberty is considered both proper and expedient. As to Class B drugs, particularly cannabis, the importation of amounts of about 20 kilogrammes will, save in the most exceptional circumstances, attract sentences of between 18 months and 3 years even if the offender be of previous excellent character. Supply of cannabis is in the 1 to 4 year bracket dependent upon scale but can be up to 10 years in serious cases. When only small amounts of cannabis are involved for personal use the offence can often be met by a fine, but if the history shows a persistent flouting of the law, imprisonment may be deemed necessary.

Customs duties on yachts

All yachts arriving in the UK are potentially liable to customs duty, but if UK built or based are normally re-admitted free of duty. Any repairs or alterations, other than ordinary running repairs, carried out abroad must be declared. If returning in a craft bought outside the country, the transaction must be disclosed. A yacht on which VAT has been paid, but which is later sold abroad, may be liable again to VAT on re-importation.

Importation

All goods and services got abroad must be disclosed; concealment may attract severe penalties. No goods should be taken ashore without the advance permission of a Customs officer. The irregular landing of goods may be regarded as smuggling, and any declaration relating to Customs which is untrue may render the goods and the vessel liable to forfeiture. An embargo applies to certain articles of a prohibited or restricted nature such as the introduction of drugs, dogs, cats, uncooked meat, listed plants, firearms, flick-knives as also pornographic material.

Rabies

Rabies is prevalent in most continental countries, spreading westward in each year, but which so far has been halted successfully by the barrier of the Channel and by preventive measures. Isolated incidents aside, the British Isles have been free from rabies since 1922. Rabies, otherwise known as hydrophobia, is a disease to which most warm-blooded animals are susceptible; it may be passed on through a bite by a dog or cat; in man it is often fatal. The law has been strengthened to prevent the introduction of rabies into the United Kingdom. The biggest threat has always been from irresponsible owners taking dogs overseas in boats, or caravans, and then trying to smuggle them back into the country. Foreign yachtsmen are frequent offenders, and profess to be unaware of the regulations and penalties.

Penalties for smuggling animals into the UK include unlimited fines and up to a year's imprisonment; in addition a destruction order of the animal may be made. The Court of Appeal has said it would have no hesitation in upholding prison sentences on persons who deliberately smuggle animals into the country. Sentimental attachment to pets cannot be allowed to excuse the infringement of a law designed to protect the public against rabies.

Under the Rabies Act 1974, as amended, strict conditions are imposed limiting the landing of designated animals by licence only. The Channel Islands, the Isle of Man, Northern Ireland and Eire are exempt. There are no legal restrictions limiting the free movement of dogs, cats and other mammals within the above places, provided that the voyage is a direct one. On his return to the UK, it is for the owner to satisfy the Customs that the animal has not been landed at any foreign port. All other animals may be landed with licence only at nominated ports and places, and must be detained in quarantine for six months (life in the case of vampire bats) at the owner's expense.

Animals from abroad on vessels in harbour must be restrained, and securely confined in a totally enclosed part of the vessel and prevented from making contact with any other animal, and in no circumstances be permitted to land. Native British animals are prohibited from boarding vessels on which there are animals from overseas.

Duty free

HM Customs permit the owner and unpaid crew of a returning yacht certain duty-free allowances, and an owner should ascertain what are the current personal concessions before departure. There are no tobacco or alcohol privileges for those under 17 years of age.

Quarantine

A yacht back from abroad is subject to public health inspection and must comply with the Public Health (Ships) Regulations. It is the responsibility of the skipper to report any case of infectious diseases to the authorities. The authorised officer of the Port Health Authority, or HM Customs and Excise Preventive Officer, if satisfied that there has been compliance with the regulations, states that he has examined the master of the yacht and has granted the vessel free pratique and gives his certificate; this must be kept on board and produced to any authorised person. If the Port Health Authority is satisfied that the master of a ship was aware, or should have been aware, of any breach of the regulations, and failed to report them, then action may be taken under the Public Health laws which may result in a fine.

Search

On coming from overseas a yacht is always liable to be boarded by Waterguard officers from the shore, or by an HM cutter on patrol, as also by coast preventive officers, or by the water police. Under the Customs and Excise Management Act 1979, where there are any reasonable grounds for supposing that a vessel may be carrying goods chargeable to any duty which has not been paid, or which are being unlawfully removed, or otherwise liable to forfeiture, any officer or constable, member of HM forces or coastguard may stop and search that vessel. The Customs give clear warning to the owners of all yachts, and other private craft, that they are liable to be searched by Customs officers in the same way as any other ship. Any craft carrying prohibited or uncustomed goods is liable to forfeiture and the persons concerned to heavy penalties.

Forfeiture

The *Taku* was an example of a yacht which infringed the law and so became forfeit. She put into Cherbourg with an American skipper wearing a white ensign. The crew, saying they were naval officers, shipped a consignment of liquor. This was transferred to another craft 17 miles off the Dorset coast, and then landed at Arne Beach, only to be intercepted inland by preventive officers. A court ruled that the *Taku* was not being used exclusively as a private yacht and, although the goods were shifted outside territorial waters, irrespective of the nationality of her owner she should be forfeit.

Customs and Excise Management Act 1979

The law as to Customs is contained in the Customs and Excise Management Act 1979, and this includes the European Communities Act 1972, which provides for co-operation between the customs services of EEC members. In any proceedings where any questions arise as to whether or not any duty has been paid on goods, or whether they have been lawfully imported, the burden of proof is on the owner.

The making of an untrue declaration or statement knowingly, or recklessly, is a serious offence. Intent to deceive is not a necessary ingredient of the offence. If any person knowingly, and with intent to defraud Her Majesty of any duty, or to evade any prohibition or restriction for the time being in force, is concerned in any fraudulent evasion, he may be liable:

(a) on summary conviction to a penalty of the prescribed sum or of three times the value of the goods, and/or to imprisonment for a term not exceeding 6 months, or to both; or

(b) on conviction on indictment to a penalty of any amount, or to imprisonment for a term not exceeding 2 years, or to both.

In addition a court may order forfeiture of the ship and costs. These financial penalties have been criticised, for they are absurdly low and, in the case of the professional smuggler, often make the game worth the candle.

Customs officers have complete discretion to compromise any legal action which may be open, and to mitigate or remit any pecuniary penalty. Thus, if an importer signs a form consenting to pay a stipulated sum by way of duty, he may be given an undertaking that proceedings will be withdrawn provided that his cheque is honoured. If he later revokes his consent the authorities may still take criminal action.

If the yacht or its furniture or effects become forfeit, the owner will look in vain to his insurers for recovery. Where a person brought into the country goods on which duty had not been paid, and these were stolen, the court declined to let him recover on the grounds that it is contrary to public policy to allow him to profit from a breach of the law.

Arrest

Police, Customs or Coastguard officers have powers of arrest without warrant, to detain any person who has committed, or whom there are reasonable grounds to suspect of having

Arrest

committed, an offence for which such person is liable to be detained under the Customs or Immigration Acts. In general, any criminal proceedings arising from a breach of the 1979 Act must be brought within 3 years.

All this is of course for the most part academic as far as the average yachtsman goes, for rarely will he cause these officials any concern. Most owners will testify that Customs officers are always most courteous, ready to impart all helpful information, and to make such concessions as their duty permits. The yachtsman is aware of the confidence which his membership of a club imports, and of the obligations which attach to any privileged ensign he may fly. He should not really have to find himself in the embarrassing position of the father of the little girl, who exclaimed excitedly while an officer was rummaging through the boat 'He's getting warmer, Mummy!'

Channel Islands

All craft visiting the Channel Islands are subject to Customs and Immigration control, which they should clear at St. Peter port, St. Helier or Gorey. Yachts arriving from foreign ports should wear a Q flat on entry. All persons leaving or joining vessels arriving from, or departing for places, other than the UK or Channel Islands, must be in possession of a valid travel document. If the speed of the vessel is in excess of 17 knots, there is a requirement of compulsory insurance if used in local waters; this is not needed for direct passages to and from the Islands. The landing of all animals from vessels arriving directly or indirectly from elsewhere other than the UK is prohibited, and very strict anti-rabies laws are enforced. All speed limits must be observed. Yachts returning to the UK from the Channel Islands, even if they have not also visited France, are subject to the same procedure as any craft arriving from foreign parts.

France

Pleasure craft entering French waters must have the correct ship's documents. The French authorities will accept a Part 1 certificate of registration, or for small yachts and motor boats under 24 metres in length, an SSR certificate. Ships owned by companies must have Part 1 official papers. If from the UK, Belgium or the Netherlands, no maritime health declaration is required. If arriving from an area of infection they should be in possession of an international certificate of vaccination.

Yachts are allowed to sail and anchor or moor along the French coast for a period of 6 months either in one or several visits over a period of 12 consecutive months. British visitors are exempt from port of call charges. A *permis de circulation* is no longer needed. There are no special concessions relating to duty-free goods and fuel. A 1976 decree bans the use of fuel domestique as a boat propellent.

Craft of under 100 tons may be boarded by French customs up to 20km from the coast to inspect ship's papers and stores. Whilst in France the boat must not be lent, chartered or used for gain without payment of import charges and taxes. Local authorities may check all craft to see that they comply with safety regulations. Navigation is restricted in certain bathing areas and motor boats must not exceed a speed of 5 knots within 300 metres of the shore save in marked boat channels.

Speed limits on inland waterways must be strictly observed. The river limits are 10–20km/h and 6–10km/h on canals. It is compulsory to wear a safety jacket going through the Rhône and Saône rivers. If water skiing, two persons must be on the trailing craft. Only those over 16 and members of an approved association or club are permitted to fish underwater.

Trailers

The maximum dimensions of vehicles and trailers are fixed by regulations and those currently in force should be consulted. If the proposed load is in excess of these dimensions, permission must be got from the Préfet of the Department of the place of entry, if this be in France.

Republic of Ireland

The formalities applicable to a boat arriving at, or departing from, Eire are almost parallel to those of the UK; for the prevailing position information should be sought from the

Secretary, Revenue Commissioners, Dublin Castle, Dublin 2.
Passports are not needed for entry, and there is no restriction on
the length of stay.

Discipline

Under the common law, a master of a British ship on the high
seas, or in a foreign port, is deemed to be standing in the
position of the head of a family. A skipper may accordingly
exercise disciplinary powers over his crew and passengers which
can extend to a right of detention in an emergency. If he
wrongly confines an alleged defaulter below decks he may be
liable to pay exemplary damages for false imprisonment. His
powers no longer allow him to compel a mutinous miscreant to
walk the plank.

7 Civil Sea Law

For they found me 'tween two drowned ones
　where the roll had landed me.
An' a four-inch crack on top of me head,
　as crazy as could be.

Rudyard Kipling
'Mulholland's Contract'

Limited liability

The civil code of the sea has much to do with the duty to take care by all ships. The legal guide lines as to this were set out in a leading case which arose from the loss of Lord Dunraven's *Valkyrie* during a Regatta held on the Clyde in 1894. Lord Dunraven was a colourful character and a central figure in yachting controversies on either side of the Atlantic. A challenger for the America's Cup, he had differences with the New York Yacht Club which he regarded as of such gravity that he briefed a barrister to represent him at an inquiry held by them. Counsel's advocacy was of no avail, for his client's name was removed from the list of members of that august body.

He was more successful in the English courts in his claim for £7500 brought against Dr Clarke, the owner of the 117 ton cutter *Satanita*. Here he alleged that in breach of a sailing rule, and as the result of improper navigation, she had run into and sunk the *Valkyrie*. The owners had signed a form which had this clause: 'I undertake that while sailing under the entry I will obey and be bound by the sailing rules of the Yacht Racing Association and the byelaws of the club'. Lord Dunraven brought proceedings for the damages which he assessed at £7500, whereas Dr Clarke contended that the sum should not exceed £8 per ton under an Act of 1862, which would have limited his liability to something of the order of £900.

The Court of Appeal held that there was a contract between the owners by which the *Satanita* was liable for all damages resulting from breach of a rule, and therefore Dr Clarke could not, as against Lord Dunraven, set up statutory limitation of liability. Lord Esher said 'I think it was very reasonable to say that if you do enter into such a game as this to be played by an incapable person, if he does commit a fault to the injury of the other, you must pay all the damages, and not be limited to £8 per ton. Otherwise, although you might have a most valuable yacht, if she were sunk by another yacht of a very small tonnage, there would be no real remedy at all. Those reasons seem to me to make the rule a most reasonable protection against gentlemen who will have their little gambol with their yachts.'

The Lords endorsed this finding, one peer saying 'I think it cannot be denied that the case of yachts is different from that of merchant vessels. Remember these are competing vessels and, where you are speaking of these first class yachts competing in a yacht race, you might as well value a race horse by its weight (so many pounds of flesh) as speak of the value of the yacht according to its tonnage'. It was confirmed that there was a contract between the owners of the damaged yachts, allowing each to sue the other and that, by agreeing to race under the YRA rules, the parties had lost their right to rely on any statutory limitation.

The question as to whether the limitation of liability privilege applies to a yacht when cruising was considered in the *Annie Hay* in 1967. This launch collided with a motor cruiser in Falmouth Harbour doing damage to the extent of £2700. The *Annie Hay* was found to be the boat at fault, and her owner tried to limit his liability under the 1894-1958 Acts to a figure under £200. The court said that he could, and so resolved the uncertainty at that time as to whether the limitation of liability rule could be successfully invoked by the owner/skipper of a yacht.

Racing

The current position as to racing is now to be found in the IYRU rules, which allow a national authority to prescribe as to damages arising from any breach of the racing rules. The RYA has decided that it was undesirable that the question of limitation of liability for yachts when racing should be different from that when they are not. It follows that under the IYRU and

RYA rules, in the event of a collision whilst racing, the owner of the infringing yacht (or his insurers) may be liable, and that such liability may be limited as provided by the Merchant Shipping Acts.

An incident where there had been a breach of the IYRU rules was the subject of litigation in 1972, which concerned a yacht race which was held under the IYRU rules. The boats were all making for the same mark when there was a collision. The court ruled that where there is an impact in a race held under IYRU rules, any breach of those rules may be a breach of contract, as each party agrees to be bound thereby; furthermore a court is not precluded by the finding of the sailing committee from dealing with any claim for damages, as the sailing committee's findings are only concerned with the question of disqualification.

Negligence

The *Seaway Code* sets out much of the philosophy of the common law and the standard of care expected of the average yachtsman. The basic legal duty is to behave reasonably. Any falling below this level may be construed as negligence by a court, making the party responsible pay for all the traceable consequences so long as they are not too remote. The law allows no leeway for amateurs afloat. A skipper is expected to behave as any reasonable mariner would do. The law requires that he display a little more knowledge of his duties than did a noble member of the Royal Yacht Squadron, Lord Cardigan, who sailed his yacht the *Enchantress* from Cowes Castle to the Crimean War to be used there as a palatial houseboat. On being asked whether he wished to take the helm he replied: 'No thank you I never take anything between meals'.

An action in negligence arises where there is a failure to use all reasonable skill that the circumstances require. The man in a dinghy may be careless if he fails to heed the danger of overhead power lines. The angler may flirt with legal disaster if he ties himself up to a channel buoy, or if he anchors so as to foul underwater pipes and cables. The man at the wheel of a speedboat, who fails to detect the declared presence of divers, may find himself presented with a heavy bill. The erratic steering of a craft towing a water skier resulting in catastrophe may prove to be both distressing and expensive. Thus a victim, who was injured by a collision with a stationary obstruction, of which the towing boat gave no notice, was able to recover substantial compensation.

It is for any person lending tools, particularly powered ones, to warn the borrower of any defects which he knows to be dangerous. Manufacturers and suppliers of goods, especially of modern glues and paints, should give warning of any danger which may result from misuse of their products. It is not enough to give directions as to use. The instructions should go on to spell out the possibilities of damage or injury which may ensue if they are ignored. A recent misuse of a fast setting adhesive, which caused a yachtsman's fingers to be stuck to such an extent that amputation was threatened, emphasises the need for all due care and caution. There is also a reported instance of a paint applied in fitting out which proved to be explosive when part-used tins were stored for too long.

To recover damages in negligence against a manufacturer the defect which caused the accident must be clearly traceable to him. Thus where a rudder failed owing to careless casting after some years of use the court rejected the claim on the footing that: 'so many contingencies must have intervened between the lack of care on the part of the makers and the casualty'.

Contributory negligence

It often occurs that an accident happens as the result of lack of care by both parties such as collisions on land or at sea. If at sea the Maritime Conventions Act 1911 applies so that if both boats are in the wrong compensation will be apportioned to the degree to which each was at fault. If on land the Law Reform (Contributory Negligence) Act provides that where both parties are to blame the damages shall be reduced to such extent as the court thinks just and equitable having regard to the claimant's share as to responsibility. Hence where a man who was working in darkness on the deck of a ship fell through an open hatch, a judge held that he was 33⅓% responsible and his award was reduced accordingly. It follows that if a person is part author of his own misfortune he cannot call on another to make good his loss in full.

Careless anchoring

A good example of where not to anchor was afforded by the ketch *Frances*. A ship was ready for launching in the Mersey, and all arrangements had been made, including the removal of a buoy in the line of the launch. Shortly before the time fixed for the ceremony, the *Frances* sailed up the river on the flood tide. Off Prince's Dock the wind dropped, and she let go her anchor which caught on the moorings of the removed buoy, and there she was held fast. A message was sent to her in these terms 'We observe that you are in the line of the launch of our *Highland Loch* and, as all preparations are made, we must launch the ship at 1230 today. We cannot be responsible for any damage done to your ship and advise you to slip your anchor and clear away at once'.

The skipper did not clear away. At 1240 a warning gun was fired and five minutes later the *Highland Loch* was duly launched; she struck the *Frances*. The first court which heard the claim for damages by the *Frances* found in her favour. The Court of Appeal upset this and said the ketch was solely to blame. They were upheld by the Lords on the footing that the shipbuilders had been placed in a dilemma as, once the blocks had been removed, it would have been dangerous to have reversed the process of launching, and they had rightly chosen the lesser of the two risks. The court thought that the skipper of the ketch was most unreasonable in refusing to move.

Careless berthing

The *Moorcock* was a ship whose name has passed into the pages of the text books as a leading case on what terms may be read properly into a contract. Whilst unloading at a jetty on the Thames, to which she had been directed, she took the ground and was damaged. The wharf owners were made to pay compensation, as it was held that it must have been an implied term of the contract that they had exercised all reasonable care in ascertaining that the bottom of the river was safe, but since the vessel settled on a ridge of high ground, clearly they had not.

Careless diving

Sub-aqua divers should abide by the BSAC code of conduct. Failure to do so, ending in disaster, may give good grounds for a claim. The blue and white flag 'A' indicating that a diver is down should be displayed and a look-out craft be in attendance. Fairways call for special care if not avoidance.

Dangerous wash

Considerations of courtesy and of the law dictate the need to avoid creating excessive wash which can damage moored craft, erode river or canal banks, endanger swimmers, and cause accidents in galleys of moored craft. There is a legal obligation when navigating not to cause danger by excessive speed and consequential wash for a person boarding another craft.

Dangerous gash

It is axiomatic that a gash bucket should not be thoughtlessly emptied over the side particularly if this contains plastic bags or sheeting which can so easily be sucked into another yacht's engine or foul the propeller so immobilising the craft.

Fire precautions

Owners should be vigilant as to gas containers and their fitting and should ensure that, where gas burners or refrigerators are fitted on their craft, the recommended practices laid down by the Ship and Boat Builders' National Federation have been followed, as also the manufacturers' instructions and, furthermore, that there has been compliance with any byelaws as to ventilation.

A couple hired a launch on the Thames which caught fire, whereupon it was found that both sand box and an extinguisher were empty. They claimed for personal injuries and loss of property. The owner blamed the hirer, who had admitted that he may have spilled petrol into the bilges when refuelling. The court, however, faulted the owner for failing to provide adequate fire fighting equipment and, in falling short of an implied obligation at law, for letting out a launch which was not reasonably fit for the purpose required.

An owner may find the Home Office publication *Fire Precautions in Pleasure Craft* of help, as would a court when assessing what precautions a reasonable skipper should take. He should evaluate those appliances which are suitable to his craft, and appreciate their effects on electrical, fibreglass and other types of fire. He should see that they are not out-dated, and should check that his crew are familiar with the drill to be carried out in the event of an emergency.

Volenti

A flag officer of the Bar Yacht Club, Sergeant Sullivan QC, was once stopped in mid-oratory in court by a judge who asked 'Has your client never heard of the doctrine of *volenti non fit injuria*?' Came the reply 'In Bantry Bay, from where my client hails, there is seldom any other topic of conversation'. The defensive doctrine of *volenti* (that to which one consents cannot be considered an injury) gives a good answer to an allegation of negligence. It means that the complainant consented with full knowledge of the risks to the doing of the act which caused his loss. Such is the lot of spectators at a motor race or an air display. Those who go to dangerous sports do so with their eyes open, and cannot succeed in a claim where an accident to themselves comes from an anticipated incident of the perilous enterprise, so long as all reasonable steps have been taken to prevent its happening, such as by fencing, stewarding and warning.

The *volenti* defence may be prayed in aid in reply to claims not only by spectators but by participants. It may apply to a boxer who is knocked out; or to a cricketer struck by a ball; or to a yachtsman hit on the head by the boom. It may relate to aquaplaners and to skin divers. Where a man assents to involvement in a hazardous activity, he cannot after be heard to complain, if despite all reasonable precautions, he is injured. In general it may be added that those who keep to the rules of their chosen sport, whether it be golfing or sailing, may expect to find judges inclined in their favour.

Crew

An owner signing on crew, in deference to the *volenti* doctrine, should impress on them any inherent risks, as also his own navigational limitations (if any), so that they cannot be heard afterwards to say that they were press-ganged into a sea venture which with hindsight they would never have freely accepted. A cautious skipper might even consider inviting a recruit to sign what submariners and the RAF call 'a blood chit'. Organisers of adventure trips should also examine the desirability of disclaiming effectively their responsibility for mishaps in the course of trips which they may plan.

Privileged wills

By the Wills Act 1837 every last will and testament, save a privileged one, must be in writing and signed by or on behalf of the testator and the signature must be made or acknowledged in the presence of two witnesses present at the same time. Few trouble to leave a will, expressing doubtless by their silence complete confidence in the statutory method of distribution laid down by the intestacy legislation. A large proportion who do it themselves by home-made wills come to grief. Indeed a special toast used to be drunk in the hall of the Law Society to such benefactors to the legal profession. A mariner or seaman at sea enjoys, like a serviceman on active service, a special privilege under the 1837 Act if he is at sea or in the course of a voyage or contemplating a fresh voyage, in that he may make a will by informal writing, or by word of mouth, or significant gesture provided that he has a testamentary intention and is supported by credible evidence. One claim to such privilege was denied by the court to the next of kin of a pilot on the Manchester Ship Canal who had inscribed his final instructions on an egg shell.

In general, in practical terms, those wishing to leave their affairs in a satisfactory state should see a solicitor.

Charts

The full area of the duty of care owed by the makers of charts and of sailing instructions is still a moot matter. As Lord Denning once said: 'A scientist or expert (including a marine hydrographer) is not liable to his readers for careless statements in his published works. He publishes the work simply for the purpose of giving information and not with any particular transaction in mind. But when a scientist, or an expert, makes an investigation and report for the very purpose of a particular transaction, in my opinion he is under a duty of care in respect of that transaction.'

In 1950 a special relationship was held to exist between the Workington Harbour and Dock Board and the owners of the *SS Towerfield*, who sought damages for her grounding in a silted channel. Admiralty publishers, at the request of the Board, had produced an inset on chart No. 1346 which showed a plan of the harbour with the channel to have a width of 250 feet. A note stated: 'In the approach channel and turning basin within the pecked lines a depth of $4\frac{1}{2}$ feet at chart datum is maintained by dredging'. It added that the plan was based on information supplied by the Board.

The supplement to the *West Coast of England Pilot* dealing with the estuary of the River Derwent read 'Less depths than $4\frac{1}{2}$ feet will be found in places: owing to the difficulty of dredging on the outer bar, depths of about 1 foot are common there'.

The trial judge found the harbour authority to blame for failing to maintain the width and depth of the channel advertised (thereby rendering the published information misleading), as also in failing to find by proper soundings what obstructions existed in the channel, and exactly where they were, and in not warning the users of the port of dangers of which the harbour authority knew, or ought to have known. In the opinion of the law lords, the Board owed a duty to warn any incoming ship whether that duty was imposed by contract or by invitation. The failure to warn the *Towerfield* had contributed to her loss.

Lord Normand thought that the soundings had been taken in a hasty and slipshod manner. He said 'The invitees are entitled to assume that the Board will exercise reasonable care to prevent peril or damage to ships resorting to the harbour from an unexpected danger of which the authorities knew, or ought to have known. I think that there was no contract, but that the Board, knowing that masters of ships would be led from their study of the chart and sailing directions to find a fairway of about the width and depth indicated, were bound to give warning of dangerous obstructions of which they were, or ought to have been aware'.

Time limits

The civil law imposes time limits within which action may be taken. In general no claim founded on the breach of an ordinary contract may be brought after six years on which the cause of complaint arose; twelve years in the case of more formal agreements made under seal. For personal injuries and death the period within which proceedings should be commenced is three years from (a) the date on which the cause of action arose, or (b) if later, the date of the plaintiff's knowledge of the facts relevant to his right of action against the defendant. Personal injuries include any disease and any impairment of a physical or mental condition.

The Maritime Conventions Act 1911 sets out special rules on the time limits as to certain marine matters and provides as follows: 'No action shall be maintainable to enforce any claim against a vessel or her owners in respect of damage done to another vessel, or any property on her, or damages for loss of life or personal injuries suffered by any person on board her, caused by the fault of the former vessel, unless proceedings are commenced within two years from the date when the damage or loss or injury was caused, provided that such a court has a discretion to extend such period to such an extent, and on such conditions, as it thinks fit'.

Burden of proof

The burden of proof in a civil action is on the complainant; it is
for him who alleged to prove affirmatively. The onus is less than
that required in a criminal matter, where the charge must be
made good beyond all reasonable doubt. The standard of proof
in actions brought for breach of contract, or of tort, is that of
proof on the balance of probabilities. If the evidence is such that
the tribunal can say 'We think it more probable than not', then
the burden is discharged; but if the probabilities are equal it is
not. There would be a *prima facie* discharge of the onus of proof
to show that a ship rammed another at her moorings in broad
light of day.

Civil proceedings

Civil proceedings may be brought in the High Court of Justice,
or in the County Courts. In general, the determining factor as to
which court resort should be made is fixed by the amount of the
claim. A High Court action usually starts by the service of a
writ, delivered personally by the plaintiff on a defendant or his
appointed agent. However, in the case of an Admiralty action
brought in certain cases against a vessel, its freight or cargo, the
writ is served on the ship itself. This procedure is normally
appropriate where claims are made in such matters as salvage,
collisions, towage and pilotage, as also mortgage or where there
is a dispute as to the possession or ownership of a vessel.

Service of such writ is carried out by affixing it for a short
time in accordance with Order 75 of the Rules of the Supreme
Court, on any mast of the ship, or on the outside of any suitable
part of the ship's superstructure, and on removing the warrant,
leaving a copy of it in a sheltered and conspicuous part of the
ship. An undertaking thereafter by the defendant to enter an
appearance may lead to a stay of any arrest of the ship; but he
may be required to furnish a sum of money by way of bail. The
average yachtsman is rarely concerned with all these complexi-
ties; clearly, if there is any hint of such involvement, or should
he return to his craft to find a writ nailed or taped to the mast, he

should take immediate steps in the direction of the nearest solicitor for competent advice.

Arbitration

Outside the ordinary courts stands arbitration. The parties to a contract are free to fix that their disputes are resolved informally by their own nominees, so avoiding what may be the unwelcome publicity and expense of the law courts. An enforceable agreement should comply with the Arbitration Act 1950, as amended, and must be in writing. Arbitration clauses are often found in contracts with insurers, partners, boat builders and repairers, and with clubs. The arbitrator should be a person who has the confidence of the parties; often the Commodore of a nominated Club, or the President of an agreed association, is invited to act. The parties may consent to an arbitrator not being bound by the ordinary strict rules of evidence.

Disputing parties naturally hope that, whether their case is conducted in the arbitration rooms, or in the ordinary courts of the realm, the adjudicator will be conversant with any technicalities which are raised. It is narrated that in the course of an 18th century trial concerning a collision, a sailor gave evidence that at the time of impact he was standing abaft the binnacle. The judge, Lord Mansfield, asked where the binnacle might be, upon which the witness who appeared to have had a rather good lunch, exclaimed 'A pretty fellow to be a judge who does not know where abaft the binnacle is'. Came the reply from the Bench 'Well, my friend, fit me for my office by telling me where abaft the binnacle is; you have already shown me the meaning of half seas over'.

8 Criminal Sea Law

Ships are but boards, sailors but men; there be
land-rats and water-rats, land-thieves and
water-thieves, I mean pirates, and then there is
the peril of waters, winds and rocks.

William Shakespeare
'The Merchant of Venice', I, iii, 22

The courts

The criminal courts take note of any offence committed within
England and Wales, or on board British ships on the high seas.
All proceedings start in the magistrates' courts. Justices of the
Peace have long been used to dealing with sailors, as is shown by
an Act of 1746 when they were empowered to fine for profane
swearing one shilling for seamen, and five shillings for
gentlemen. Summary offences are dealt with the Justices, but if
the matter is of any gravity then it is referred by them to the
Crown Court to be decided by a judge and jury. One of their
curious powers, more of a civil than a criminal nature, stems
from the poor laws of the middle ages enabling them to deal
with defaulting ratepayers. Fortunately for yachtsmen, government proposals for the rating of swinging moorings have so far
been successfuly resisted.

Today's magistrates are like Caesar's wife, above suspicion. It
was not always so. In 1767 a citizen confronted with a gang
smuggling kegs of brandy ashore at Padstow exclaimed: 'Have
you no shame? Is there no magistrate at hand? Cannot any
Justice of the Peace be found in this fearful county?' Came the
reply: 'Yes, he is over there holding the lantern'.

Serious offences such as murder, rape, piracy or supplying
dangerous drugs are investigated by the magistrates, who
commit the accused for trial by jury if satisfied that a *prima facie*
case has been established. Medium matters, including assaults
and criminal damage, may permit of an election either by the
prosecution, or the defendant, as to whether the mode of trial be
summarily before the Justices or be sent for consideration by

121

the Crown Court. Taking a boat without authority is an example of an offence which can be tried either way; it carries a maximum penalty of £2000, or up to 6 months' imprisonment on a summary trial, and of up to 3 years' imprisonment, and an unlimited fine, on conviction after a trial on indictment before the Crown Court.

Foreign law

Happily for those who take to the waters in small boats, the criminal code is not so strict towards sailors on the sea as it is towards drivers on the road. In the main Parliament has pursued a policy of *laisser faire* in relation to the small time seafarer, aiming rather to educate than to legislate. Our European link may yet bring about change. In France, pleasure craft are classified and their cruising range accordingly limited from 5 nautical miles off the shore to an unrestricted distance. Dinghies are barred from going more than 2 miles out and from night navigation. In the USA the Federal Boat Safety Act lays down basic requirements. To row an unlighted dinghy from ship to shore at night without a lifejacket adds up to two offences, for which the hapless mariner may be fined 100 dollars apiece.

Navigation

On the rights or otherwise of navigation, the courts have had their say, as is illustrated by the complaint which was brought before the Liskeard Justices against a spectator alleged to have broken a ban on all movement in Looe harbour during a Regatta, by being 100 yards upstream from the races. He was convicted and fined, but vindicated on appeal. Here it was stated that the function of a Harbour Master was akin to that of a policeman controlling traffic; whereas in certain circumstances it might be necessary to impose a comprehensive ban, in this particular case it was unreasonable to impose a total ban on all movement because of the possibility of interference with rowers competing over 800 yards of harbour space.

A yachtsman on passage from Littlehampton to Bembridge

had a headache, so he put into the tidal harbour of Pagham where he anchored, planning to stay overnight. He was unaware that Pagham, as a nature reserve, came under the National Parks and Access to the Countryside Act of 1949, and that local bye-laws prohibited launching, mooring or leaving any boat within the reserve. On arrival he was hailed by a warden and asked if he was in distress. On giving a negative reply, he was asked to leave forthwith, but despite favourable conditions, this he declined to do. He appeared before the Chichester Justices charged with mooring his boat in a reserve without reasonable excuse. He was convicted and fined £5 and ordered to pay £50 costs.

The yachtsman appealed to the Divisional Court, arguing that he had not broken the bye-laws for he had anchored and not moored. Alternatively he asserted that there was a public right of way in tidal waters. On the first point there was much discussion as to the meaning of the word 'moored'. Did it include anchoring? Various dictionaries were examined which showed that mooring 'embraces the use of the ship's own anchors and cables'. The court ruled that the meaning of an ordinary word in the English language is not a matter of law but of fact, and if the justices had found that the yacht remained at anchor, although sometimes grounded, it was impossible to say that their conclusion that the yacht was anchored was wrong, and accordingly the yachtsman lost his appeal.

On the point that there was a public right of navigation in tidal waters, the court approved this earlier judicial dictum. 'The rights of navigation are analogous to the rights of the public on a highway on land; that is to say, the right of coming and going and doing those things incidental thereto. On a highway I may stand still for a reasonably short time, but I must not put my bed upon the highway and permanently occupy a portion of it. I may stoop to tie up my shoelace, but I must not occupy a pitch and invite people to come upon it and have their hair cut. I may let my van stand long enough to deliver and load books, but I must not turn my van into a permanent stall. In the same way, so far as navigation is concerned, I may have to wait for a favourable wind, I may have to load or discharge cargo, and I may have to do repairs necessary or desirable before again setting out to sea, but I may not permanently occupy a part of the water over a foreshore, even if I am doing something which incidentally assists the navigation of others'.

Manslaughter

In the time honoured definition, first laid down by Lord Hale, the crime of manslaughter is committed where a person of sound mind and discretion unlawfully kills any reasonable creature under the Queen's peace, the death following within a year and a day. Gross mismanagement of a boat by the person in charge whereby it is upset and an occupant drowned is manslaughter, so too a bathing fatality caused by a ski helmsman recklessly buzzing a boat at anchor.

Dangerously unsafe ship

Section 44 of the Merchant Shipping Act 1979 provides that if a ship in a port in the UK is, having regard to the nature of the service for which she is intended, unfit to go to sea without serious danger to limb or life an offence is committed. No proceedings may be brought without the consent of the Secretary of State or of the Director of Public Prosecutions. No such consent, however, is required where there is a breach of a bye-law, and so an owner who brought a hulk into Ilfracombe for repairs was said to have been rightly convicted for failing to remove a vessel which was 'laid by or neglected as fit for sea service'.

Submarine cables

By the Submarine Telegraph Act 1885 any person who unlawfully and wilfully, or by culpable negligence breaks or injuries any submarine cable (to which a Convention of 1884 applies) in such a manner as to interrupt or obstruct in whole or in part telegraphic communications, may be liable to imprisonment for 3 months in the event of culpable negligence, and for 5 years otherwise. It is a defence to show that damage arose from seeking to preserve life or limb, or preserving the vessel, and that all reasonable precautions had been taken to avoid injury.

Nevertheless an owner may still be found liable in civil terms. Thus where a ship fouled an electricity submarine cable between Skye and the mainland when changing her position in a storm, the master was found to be responsible as she had been allowed to drag anchor in a place where there was a known cable.

False signals

Sea marks have always loomed large in the eye of the law as is seen in an Act of Elizabeth in 1566 which ran: 'Forasmuch as by the destroying and taking away of certain steeples, woods and other marks standing upon the main shores of the realm as beacons and marks of ancient times accustomed for seafaring men divers ships have by the lack of such marks of late years been lost in the sea anyone removing the said marks shall be subject to a fine of £100 or to outlawry'.

Under the Malicious Damage Act 1861 a court has a discretion to impose imprisonment for life where any person unlawfully masks, or removes any light or signal, or exhibits any false light or signal, with intent to bring any boat into danger. This is a hangover from the heyday of smuggling, rife in the west country where a Cornish jury would never convict. The Reverend Troutbeck is long remembered in those parts for proclaiming from his pulpit: 'We pray Thee O Lord not that wrecks should happen, but if they do that Thou will guide them to the Scilly Isles for the benefit of the poor inhabitants'.

Buoys

The same Act makes it an offence punishable by a term of imprisonment, not exceeding 7 years, unlawfully to cut away, cast adrift, remove alter, deface, sink, or destroy any boat, buoy, buoy-rope, perch or mark, used or intended for the guidance of seamen for the purpose of navigation.

Public Health Acts

The Public Health Acts 1897 to 1961 allow local authorities to make bye–laws to ensure good and orderly conduct of persons in charge of pleasure boats. These may provide that, for the prevention of danger, obstruction or annoyance to persons bathing in the sea or using the seashore, speed restrictions may be imposed, and an insistence made as to proper silencers. These regulations may be effective up to 1000 yards from low watermark at ordinary spring tides, and the speed limit is normally in the region of 8 knots. Fines may be inflicted for dangerous, careless, or inconsiderate navigation.

Foreshore

To what extent does bathing from the shore, or in the sea, add up to an unlawful obstruction, or to an act of trespass? The answer was given over a century ago that the public have no common law right to use the shore, or to pass and re-pass to bathe in the sea on what may be the property of the Queen, or a private owner. This was all set out in an old case in which some boys had gone over a beach on the Isle of Thanet to swim. The judge said 'By the common law all royal subjects have in general a right of passage over the sea with vessels, for the purpose of navigation, and have *prima facie* a common of fishery there, and they have the same rights over that portion of the sea which lies over the foreshore at the time when the foreshore is covered with water. But when the sea recedes and the foreshore becomes dry there is not, as I understand the law, any general common law right in the public to pass over the foreshore. There are certain limited rights in the public to pass over the foreshore, and the fact that such limited rights exist goes to show that there cannot be a general right. For purposes of navigation there exists a common law right to cross the foreshore in order to launch a boat. The right of navigation, it has been said, is for the general benefit of all the kingdom, and the right of fishing tends to the sustenance and beneficial enjoyment of individuals, and for these purposes it would seem that there are special rights to cross the foreshore for all purposes.'

However, the shore owner should avoid over-zealous action. Thus where, in the 1930s, the forthright landlady of Brownsea Island carried out her threat 'If you come here again my servants have orders to throw you, or anybody belonging to you, into the sea', it was not altogether surprising that the magistrates fined her £2 for assault.

Trespassers

In 1935 a landlord sued trespassers who had opened locked gates and followed a footpath to the sea. Evidence was given that visitors to Abersoch for many years had claimed that in doing so they were simply exercising a right of way. The court held that the public had no right to use the shore for bathing and were trespassing; even if this be tolerated by the Crown, there was certainly no right in the public to pass to and fro over the beach for all purposes. However, it may be that there was a right for fishermen to cross the shore to launch a boat, and that there was a right for all to land in peril or necessity.

'Trespassers will be prosecuted' signs may, for the most part, be described as wooden lies. Trespass (which is an entry without legal right on the land of another) is a wrong for which civil proceedings may be brought. Prosecution only arises in the event of criminal conduct such as entry as a trespasser on property with an intent to do damage or to steal. However, trespass on Ministry of Defence or other protected property may also be a criminal offence. It is also an offence under the Official Secrets Acts to go into any prohibited place which includes any work of defence, arsenal, naval or airforce establishment or station, factory, dockyard, minefield, camp, ship or aircraft belonging to the Crown. The Atomic Energy Act 1954, and the Nuclear Installation Act 1965, make similar provisions.

In ordinary cases of civil trespass, the proper drill is to ask the intruder for his name and address so that remedy may be got in the county court. He should then be told to leave and, if he refuses, the owner is entitled to use a reasonable degree of force to expel him; any excessive use of force would be an unjustifiable criminal assault. The law of trespass applies to land and not to boats. At the same time a person has clearly no right to set foot without permission of the owner aboard the craft of another, save in an emergency where he would be sanctioned by necessity. Where boats are rafted alongside it must be that implied permission may be assumed, according to the customs of seamen, to cross adjoining craft, provided this is done with all due care and courtesy. Anyone doing so must take the place as he finds it, and there is in general no duty to make good any damage he may suffer when availing himself of this implied licence. It is courteous to cross another boat forward of her mast and not to clamber over the cockpit and gape into the saloon.

Banned areas

In seamanlike terms, the art of navigation is an ability to conduct a ship from one spot on the earth's circumference to another by sea expeditiously and safely. It calls for a knowledge of the places where a boat may not by law go. Thus, save in an unavoidable emergency, a ship must not stray into the perimeters of oil rigs or firing ranges, or tie up at channel buoys or lighthouses, or ground on oyster beds or foul trawling nets, or anchor over submarine cables or gas lines. Any restrictions imposed by the MOD or harbour authorities must be observed. The Protection of Wrecks Act 1973, and orders made thereunder, secure the protection of sites of historic wrecks and sunken treasure and make restriction orders on parts of the sea within the seaward limits of UK territorial waters.

Oil rigs

The limits set by the Continental Shelf Act 1964 give effect to the Geneva Convention on the High Seas of 1958. It provides for the exploration and exploitation of the shelf and confers rights which the UK is entitled to exercise outside its own waters as to the sea bed and sub-soil. Under this and other measures, such as the Oil and Gas Enterprise Act 1982, safety zone orders may be made prohibiting ships on penalty of fine and/or imprisonment imposed on the owner or master, from entering certain areas without permission. Boats tacking around oil rigs should take note for the onus is on the trespasser to prove that he did not, and would not on reasonable inquiry, know that the area was out of bounds.

An Admiralty Notice to Mariners warns that close approach by yachts to oil rigs, etc. (which may include unmarked submerged obstructions) can be extremely dangerous to the yacht and to the rig. It advises mariners to assume the existence of a safety zone extending to a distance of 500 metres around installations measured from the outer edges, and to keep outside such zone.

Joy riding

Up to 1968 there was a gap in the criminal law which left uncovered the unauthorised taking of a pleasure craft for joy riding or other purposes. This was put right by the Theft Act 1968 which equated the taking of a pleasure, or other craft, to that of a motor vehicle. The Theft Act now makes it an offence for a person, without the consent of the owner, or of other lawful authority, to take a conveyance for his own or another's use or, knowing that any conveyance has been taken without such authority, to drive it or to allow himself to be carried in it. It is a defence for a person to show that he had in fact lawful authority, or that he would have the owner's consent if the owner knew of his actions. A 'conveyance' is defined as any conveyance constructed, or adapted, for the carriage of a person, or persons, whether by land, water or air. A recent authority emphasises that this does not include a horse!

One of the earliest cases tried under the new law was that of a youth who removed an inflatable from a lifeboat depot and drove it away on a trailer. He was convicted but he appealed, arguing that to complete such an offence there must be some element of propulsion in its own element namely water. The court said that the statute contained no requirement of actual driving away and that propulsion was not necessary to complete the offence.

A later appellant was more successful. He boarded a launch aware that it had been taken without authority. Was he rightly found guilty of aiding and abetting in this venture? He had looked forward to a joy ride which was frustrated because the craft did not actually move. His appeal was allowed on the basis that to be carried involved some movement, which was absent here.

Criminal damage

Although casting a craft adrift may not amount to the offence of taking a conveyance without authority, it may come under the Criminal Damage Act of 1971. This makes it an offence punishable by 10 years' imprisonment for a person 'who, without lawful excuse, destroys or damages any such property belonging to another, intending to destroy or damage any such property, or being reckless as to whether any such property would be destroyed or damaged'. It is open to the Crown Court to award compensation to the victim, but this it is generally reluctant to do where the offender is to go to prison and there is no evidence as to ability to pay. In these circumstances the injured party, or his insurers, may have to look in the direction of the civil courts.

In 1965 the yacht *Silver Mist* was moored off Brownsea Island in Poole Harbour. On the island there was a party of Borstal boys on training exercise. They evaded their warders and boarded a boat, casting her adrift so that she ran into the *Silver Mist* and caused much damage. The action brought by her owners the Dorset Yacht Company against the Home Office raised complex issues which were eventually argued in the Lords. The Home Office had disclaimed liability, but the finding of the law lords was that the supervising officers, being aware of the presence of the craft offshore, had failed to display reasonable control over their charges; this allowed the owner to recover from that department.

Managers of marinas and yacht havens can make their contribution to the reduction of crime by posting up prominent notices designed to deter villains and vandals. Such notices could *inter alia* indicate that there is a severe penalty of imprisonment for cutting away, casting adrift or defacing or damaging any boat.

Lobster pots

The behaviour of a few divers in submerging close to lobster and crab pots has given rise to anger among some fishermen. Pot markers are attractive to the diver because they denote rocky ground; they are also a target for unscrupulous French trawlers. A Southern Fisheries Officer recently informed his committee at Bournemouth that there was widespread concern at the taking of lobsters out of pots in that area, and that interlopers could be killed at the hands of irate fishermen if legislation were not introduced to prevent larceny! The Sub-Aqua Club enjoins all divers as part of their code of conduct to keep clear of buoys, pots and pot markers. Yachtsmen, who cannot be absolved entirely from incidents causing damage to this gear, would also wish to conform with such good advice.

Oyster beds

The Sea Fisheries Acts 1967–81 seek to protect private oyster beds and make it a criminal offence to disturb or injure in any manner any shellfish bed or fishery except for a lawful purpose of navigation or anchorage. In addition to a fine, compensation may be ordered. Anti-fouling paints can pose their problems which have led manufacturers over the years to withdraw arsenic and mercury compounds which tend to endanger the environment. The Ministry of Agriculture, Fisheries and Food have concluded that tin compounds leeching from pleasure boat hulls have caused deformation in oysters, and they are empowered to make regulations whereby retailers, boatyards and tradesmen, if in breach, may be liable on summary conviction to a fine of £2000.

Crime prevention

The nautical crime wave of theft and vandalism is continually rising. There is a steady call in criminal circles for boating accessories and navigational equipment. Outboards, radar, portable TVs, DFs, compasses, sextants, logs, liferafts, trailers etc, are all expensive items much in demand. Some crooks steal to order. Others often try to get rid of their ill-gotten gains in the local inn or by advertisement in a local paper. Anyone offered goods at low cost from an unknown source should be on guard. Section 22 of the Theft Act 1968 runs 'A person handles stolen goods if (otherwise than in the course of the stealing) knowing or believing them to be stolen goods he dishonestly receives the goods, or dishonestly undertakes or assists in their retention, removal, disposal or realisation by or for the benefit of another person, or if he arranges to do so'. Quite apart from the criminal implications of receiving, a civil consequence of such an unfortunate acquisition may lead to the return of the tainted property to its true owner. Discovery of missing property is often made when equipment such as liferafts and DFs have been sent to the manufacturers in all innocence for servicing.

The police rightly urge all skippers to do their best to make their craft secure against crime. The first line of defence is a good lock, making sure that the key is not left aboard in the owner's absence. An extra safeguard may be an anti-theft alarm device. Ideally, outboards, liferafts and safety gear should be kept below behind shut curtains when a boat is unattended. If left on deck all kit should be secured properly where possible. In any event the dinghy, liferaft and lifebuoys should be marked clearly with the ship's name. A note should be entered in the log, and a duplicate kept, of the make and serial mark of the outboard, liferaft and inflatable. Valuable portable equipment should be taken ashore where practicable and in any event when the boat is laid up, and then not left on public view in a car, but secured out of sight in the boot. Windsurfers' boards are particularly at risk and when in transit should be locked on to a secure roof rack. Photographs should be taken of any unusual items of value and full details recorded. The magnification of binoculars should be noted, as also the lens number of a camera. Where possible the name of the owner or ship should be marked inside such articles as the ship's clock, barometer, echo sounders, flashlights and other equipment, to assist in identification.

Skippers should also indulge in mutual aid, and be conscious of their neighbours and report anything suspicious to the berth or harbour master, or to the police. A record should be made in the log, or some other form, so that the owner can pass on to the authorities information along these lines:

(1) Where and when the incident happened.
(2) The number of persons involved.
(3) Description.
(4) Name of any boat, or registration mark of any vehicle.
(5) All other relevant details including any clues which may be of forensic scientific value on the principle that every contact leaves a trace, e.g. fingerprints, shoe prints, tyre and tool marks, traces of paint, glass, fibres, cosmetics etc.

Arrest

At common law the ordinary citizen has a power to arrest any person committing a breach of the peace in his presence. By the Criminal Law Acts of 1966 and 1977 any person may arrest without warrant anyone whom he suspects with reasonable cause to be in the act of committing an arrestable offence, i.e. one which carries with it a sentence of 5 years or more imprisonment. He should thereafter deliver the offender to a constable. A skipper is empowered by necessity to preserve the safety of his ship and of his passengers, and accordingly if he has reasonable ground to believe such detention to be essential for upholding good order and discipline, he may so act. He is not bound to wait for an actual mutiny. He may intercept any steps towards it on the part of passengers or crew. But the crux of the matter is that there must be some act calculated in the anticipation of a reasonable man to interfere with the safety, or the due preservation, of the voyage.

Nuisance

At common law a public nuisance, which is a criminal offence, is any act or omission which endangers the life, health, property, morals or comfort of the public, or obstructs them in the exercise or enjoyment of rights common to all subjects. The annoyance may arise from noise or stench, or any interference with public comfort or convenience. Inordinate battery charging activities; excessive decibel ratings caused by power-boats; loud playing of radios and musical instruments at a late hour; inconsiderate discharge of exhaust fumes, may all raise an inquiry under this head, as does unauthorised obstruction of the fairway. The erection of an embankment in a harbour hampering the public right of navigation has been declared a public nuisance; nor is it a defence to claim that this was of advantage to other uses of the port. Burial at sea is a permitted practice but this must be done without creating a nuisance.

The Prevention of Oil Pollution Act 1971 prohibits the discharge of oil or oil mixture into any part of the sea. It is a defence to shew that the escape was consequential on damage to the vessel and that all reasonable preventive steps were taken. It is contrary to the Dumping at Sea Act 1974 to dump substances or articles over the side into the sea without licence, or otherwise than for the purpose of securing the safety of the ship. A discharge incidental to the normal operation of the ship is permissible.

Births and deaths

Under the Merchant Shipping (Return of Births and Deaths) Regulations a report must be made in writing as soon as practicable to the Registrar General of any birth or death on a British sea-going ship. Failure to do so is punishable by a fine. A British ship whether on the high seas, or sailing in foreign territorial waters is deemed at law to be part of the soil of England and anyone born aboard is *prima facie* a British subject.

Blight by boats

An Englishman's home is today no longer his castle. Various officials now have rights to enter private property to see if there have been any infringements of statutory regulations, and if so, in certain cases, to bring offenders before the criminal courts. The building of boats in gardens, and the laying up of family cruisers in back yards, have caused concern to some councils. Some local authorities seek powers from Parliament to ban the keeping on private property of certain heavy commercial vehicles, loose boxes, caravans and boats. One school of thought is that such rights seem to be unnecessary in view of the ability to deal with bad cases of blight as a public nuisance.

One householder who built a ferro-cement craft in his front garden got a letter from the Director of Planning which read 'The Council's solicitors say that the long term construction of a boat of this size, with its supporting structure and scaffolding, in the curtilage of an ordinary house in a residential area, constitutes a development under section 22 of the Town and Country Planning Act 1971 and you are accordingly requested to remove it forthwith'.

Firearms

By section 13 of the Firearms Act 1968, a person may without certificate have in his possession a firearm, or ammunition, on board a ship, or a signalling apparatus, or ammunition as part of the equipment of the ship and, if he has obtained from the police a permit for the purpose, he may remove these from the vessel.

In any event a yachtsman should out of caution consider applying for a certificate from the Chief Officer of Police for the area in which he resides as this will cover all eventualities and is available without charge for a period of three years. A 'firearm' means a lethal barrelled weapon of any description from which any shot, bullet, or any other missile such as a rocket or flare can be discharged. Those in possession of Verey pistols should also apply for a free certificate. In 1830 the lock keeper at Teddington made a request to the Commissioners to be allowed to keep a blunderbuss, a bayonet and a pair of pistols to defend himself against rogues and vagabonds. Still rife though these may be, it is doubtful if such a demand would be considered sympathetically today.

Certain distress signals can pose legal problems if taken ashore during laying up, and when there is doubt application should be made to the police. Yacht clubs should check that they hold proper authority for any starting gun or ammunition on their premises.

Fishery limits

Fishery limits claimed by the UK are more a matter of concern for aliens than for patrials who have a right to fish in tidal waters. By the Fishery Limits Act 1976 the fishing limits of the British Isles were extended from 12 to 200 miles from the baselines from which the breadth of the territorial sea is measured. It will be recalled that at a time of EEC negotiations as to a common policy, a Danish skipper, Mr Kent Kirk, was convicted in 1983 at Newcastle Crown Court for trawling off the NE coast. Later the European court at Luxembourg ruled there was then a vacuum in the regulations and that there was no way in which a Community member could ban co-members from its coastal zone.

Radio

Radiotelephone apparatus on small craft comes under the control of the Wireless Telegraphy Act 1949 as amended. This provides that any person who installs or uses any apparatus for wireless telegraphy on a British ship, whether registered or not, except under and in accordance with a licence, shall be guilty of an offence. All equipment must be of a type currently approved by the Department of Trade and Industry. The penalty for infringement is a fine and/or imprisonment of up to 3 months. It may be that some yachtsmen are unwittingly infringing regulations which may render them liable to criminal prosecution and in the event of doubt or difficulty they would do well to refer any problems for proper advice to the Licensing Branch of the Radio Regulatory Division at the Department of Trade and Industry, Waterloo House from whom licences are obtained. A useful guide for maritime radio users is set out by British Telecom International in their publiction *Maritime Radio Services for Yachts and Other Small Craft*. There are various categories of licence as follows:

A Ship Wireless Licence authorising the establishment and use of a sending and receiving station. A hand-held distress radio telephone with a call/receiver capacity, fixed tuned to 2182 kHz frequency does not require a licence; but a fixed apparatus would.

A Ship (Receiving Only) Licence authorising the establishment and use of a receiving station for receiving messages from coast and certain other radio stations, in addition to the reception of normal broadcast programmes. Coastal stations transmit traffic lists, navigation warnings, weather bulletins and gale warnings. An unfixed Radio Direction Finder does not fall within the mischief of the licensing provisions; nor is a licence needed for an ordinary hand portable radio receiving set.

A Ship (Emergency Only) Licence authorising the installation of a fixed sending and receiving station for use only in emergency.

Private VHF Stations (Yachts) operated by clubs and marinas require a separate licence in addition to a Ship licence and this enables communications limited to the business of the club or marina but must not be used for intership working.

Not only must every radiotelephone apparatus on vessels be licensed but they may only be used by a person holding a certificate of competence in radiotelegraphy or under his supervision. Such certificates are issued to persons of any nationality if they pass an examination administered by the RYA. In general the authority to operate radiotelephone equipment on board United Kingdom registered vessels is granted only to British subjects, British protected persons and citizens of the Irish Republic.

A ship licence does not cover the reception of TV programmes, and for this a separate Television Broadcasting Receiving licence is required for any such set used; save that where an owner already holds a TV licence in respect of his residence he may use a portable receiving set otherwise than at those premises, provided that the set is operated by batteries wholly contained in the set, and is not permanently installed in any place other than his home.

By section 5 of the Wireless Act, any person who sends any message which to his knowledge is false or misleading, and in particular any message which falsely suggests that a vessel is in distress, or in need of assistance, or is not in distress or not in need of assistance, is guilty of an offence.

The Merchant Shipping (Safety Convention) Act 1949 makes it obligatory to render assistance to vessels in distress on receiving at sea a signal of distress, or information from any source that a vessel or aircraft is in distress. Another Convention of 1932 makes it an offence for a master to fail to report dangerous ice, dangerous derelicts, and any other direct danger to navigation. The penalty for this failure is a fine.

CB radio

By section 1 of the 1949 Act it is an offence to install or use Citizen Band radio apparatus other than in accordance with a CB licence. The use of this may also be subject to local regulations including planning restrictions and bye-laws. No transmission which is grossly offensive or of an indecent or obscene character may be sent, nor may goods or services be advertised. The CB Code of Practice can be got from any Post Office, as also a licence available to any one aged 14 or over. CB is not a substitute for Channel 16 and though a useful aid to the yachtsman is subject to severe limitations as far as small craft go.

EPIRB

Emergency Position Indicating Radio Beacons operating on 121.5MHz and 243MHz need a licence. They can prove a valuable guide to detection in every sense of the term as one possessor of such found out to his surprise. A radio ham enthusiast in Nice intercepted a Mayday signal coming from the North of England. He alerted the authorities. The transmission was tracked down to a house in Newcastle-on-Tyne. There in a cupboard was found the responsible apparatus, as also a haul of marine equipment, which had been stolen from a local chandlery. The astonished culprit was duly convicted at the Crown Court where he discovered that the lack of a licence was the least of his troubles.

Duty to assist

Section 6 of the Maritime Conventions Act 1911 provides that the master, or person in charge of a vessel, shall so far as he can do so without serious danger to his own vessel, her crew and passengers (if any) render assistance to every person, even if such person be a subject of a foreign state at war with Her Majesty, who is found at sea in danger of being lost, and if he fails to do so he shall be guilty of a crime.

A master is discharged from a duty to give aid as soon as he is aware that another ship is standing by, or is informed by the master of any ship which has reached those in distress that assistance is no longer needed.

A century ago the courts ruled that shipwrecked mariners from the yacht *Mignonette* who took to an open boat on the high seas and, after 18 days adrift, killed and ate a youth so as to survive, were guilty of murder. They had set up the defence of necessity and sought to rely on an American authority which had sanctioned the throwing overboard of passengers in order to lighten the load of a ship in distress. Lord Coleridge in rejecting this proposition declared that English law would have none of this. He said to preserve life is generally a duty but that it may be the plainest and highest duty to sacrifice it. He likened the duty of a captain to his crew to that as illustrated in the noble case of the *Birkenhead* and went on: 'Was it more necessary to kill the youth than those of the grown men? The answer is "No".' Quoting from *Paradise Lost* he added:

'So spoke the Fiend, and with necessity,
The tyrant's plea, excused his devilish deed.'

The court then proceeded to pass sentence of death upon the prisoners but this was later commuted by Queen Victoria to 6 months imprisonment. It is on record that a group of sympathisers planned to give a banquet upon their release but were unable to agree on the nature of the victuals to be supplied. W.S. Gilbert was inspired by this macabre incident to pen 'The Yarn of the *Nancy Bell*':

For I loved the cook as a brother, I did
And the cook he worshipped me;
But we'd both be blowed, if we'd either be stowed
In the other chap's hold, you see.

9 Boats on Wheels

He wandered down the mountain grade
Beyond the speed assigned –
A youth whom Justice often stayed
And generally fined.
He went alone that none might know
If he could drive or steer.
Now he is in the ditch, and Oh!
The differential gear!

Rudyard Kipling
'The Idiot Boy'

Law on wheels

Those who go down to the sea and mess about in boats have, when they get there, more in mind the rules of the waves than those of the shore. One of the joys of going afloat is to be free, like a citizen of Venice or Sark, from the tyranny of the motor car. Here a skipper need have no fear of scoring traffic penalty points, or having his licence endorsed or revoked. His main link with his parked car may be that he has taken its battery aboard on the principle that it is seamanlike to have spares of everything, with the added bonus of leaving an immobilised vehicle ashore. Some fanatics, whom those who deal in marine equipment may applaud, go so far as to advocate in the interests of safety that every craft should have a duplicate in tow! There must be few, if any, eccentrics of this ilk, but there are many who do have to tow their boats to and fro on land (complete with spare bulbs, tyres and wheel bearings) and who are concerned with what the law has to say about trailers.

Trailer law

The law is not easy to trace or to state. In one case, *Lyon* v. *Oxford* 1983 RTR 257, about a trailer with two axles 34 inches apart being driven on the M6 at 65 mph there was a dispute as to whether the 40 or 60 mph restriction was applicable. Mr Justice Forbes said: 'The Ministry of Transport itself acknowledges that apparently there is considerable difficulty in arriving at any sensible conclusion as to what the regulation means and they hope to get it right the next time the regulations are amended.' In the light of the ambiguous nature of the statutory provisions, he adopted a construction which was more beneficent than malign to the motorist. Long gone is the alleged attitude of the late 1940s to the effect that they knew all about the law in the Department and the public found out soon enough in the police courts!

The rules of the road are contained *inter alia* in the intricate provisions of the Road Traffic Regulations Act 1967, the Road Traffic Acts 1972 and 1974, the Transport Acts 1980 and 1981, as also the Motor Vehicles (Construction and Use) Regulations 1978 as amended and the Motor Vehicles (Variation of Speed Limits) Regulations. All such legislation is under constant change, especially under EEC pressure towards harmonisation. The law as to road traffic competes with that of liquor licensing in complexity. It has been said that to get good advice on the latter the best plan is to ask a publican. It may be equally true that to be properly apprised as to the former it may be as well to ask a traffic policeman. Certainly if in doubt or difficulty an inquiry to such organisations as the RAC, AA, CSMA or RYA may help. AA Legal Services supply a most useful leaflet entitled *The Law About Trailers* to members containing a synopsis of the more important provisions applicable to motor cars in Great Britain. They caution that the law in both Northern Ireland and the Republic of Ireland may contain different provisions. Practical tips as to the towing of a small sailing cruiser on a trailer behind a family car are given in a helpful book by Jacey Winters, *Trail & Sail* (Nautical Books, 1981). The *AA Illustrated Guide to Britain's Coast* (1984) is most informative as to the location of launching ramps or slipways for trailer-borne craft.

On the road

The Road Traffic Acts only apply to the use of a vehicle on a road. By section 96 of RTA 1972, a road is defined as 'any highway and any other road to which the general public has access and includes bridges over which a road passes'. A quay at Newcastle where the public were free to walk or motor and where there was no notice of hindrance to stop them, has been held to be a road. On the other hand, an occupation road leading to a marina at the entrance of which is a sign prohibiting trespassers would not be a public road as its access is restricted to a limited class of user.

In Alan Herbert's misleading case of *Rumpheimer v. Haddock* it will be recalled that the plantiff was driving his car along the flooded Chiswick Mall when he met the defendant paddling a small boat in the opposite direction. Here the law of the road was in conflict with that of the sea. 'Port to port, you fool!' Haddock cried to no avail. The court found the motorist at fault on the footing that at the material time the road was in fact a waterway. Sailor trailers on a wet motorway would be advised not to rely on their self-steering gear, but to follow the rules set out in the *Highway Code* and maintain proper lane discipline by keeping to the left and not using the right-hand lane of a three lane carriageway unless there are exceptional circumstances. Few things terrify the ordinary motorist more than being pursued by a yacht on a trailer being towed by some lesser breed without the law trying to overtake at 80 mph – save perhaps a mobile crane.

Trailer

The Acts apply to the use of vehicles and trailers on a road. By section 190 of RTA 1972 a motor vehicle is any mechanically propelled vehicle intended or adapted for use on roads. A trailer is defined as 'a vehicle drawn by a motor vehicle'. The Divisional Court confronted with a poultry shed fitted with iron bogie wheels which was being towed along the road for sale at a market in Norfolk found this to be a trailer. It follows for the purpose of the Act that a trailer means anything on wheels drawn by a motor vehicle and it has been held that wheels include roller skates!

Insurance and test certificate

Section 143 of RTA 1972 requires every person who uses, or causes, or permits, another person to use a motor vehicle on a road to have a policy of insurance in respect to third party risks and in evidence thereof is under an obligation to produce a certificate in the prescribed form if so required. Failure to be insured may lead to a fine, endorsement, 4–8 penalty points and, if deliberate, disqualification. A motorist if towing should check with care to see that he is covered for this specific operation. If in any doubt he should ask his insurance company, for some policies exclude cover of an insured vehicle whilst it has a trailer attached thereto. He should not take it for granted that he is, or that any policy he has extends to anyone he permits to take the steering wheel. It should also be appreciated that separate arrangements will need to be made as to the boat, and that though there is no compulsory requirement of insurance of the boat, for his own peace of mind he will wish (unless he wants to be his own insurer) that the risk is looked after either by his boat or car insurers. A current MOT test certificate is required by the Motor Vehicles (Tests) Regulations for every car first registered more than 3 years previously but this does not apply to the ordinary trailer itself. Non-commercial trailers require no Road Fund Licence.

Learners and passengers

By the MV (Driving Licences) Regulations 1976 the holder of a provisional licence, i.e. a learner, is not allowed to drive a vehicle which is towing a trailer. There is a ban on the carriage of passengers on a trailer. A skipper should ensure that no stowaways have sneaked aboard. In some cases a passenger must be present in the towing vehicle and this is mandatory where a load projects over 3.05 metres.

Immobilising detached trailer

Trailers when detached should be securely anchored. By Regulation 127 of MV (C&U) Regulations 1978, no person in charge of a trailer shall cause or permit such trailer to stand when detached from the drawing vehicle unless one at least of its wheels is prevented from revolving by the setting of a brake or the use of a chain chock or other device. Even off a public road this safeguard should be followed, for if a trailer was to run amuck in a dinghy park in the event of disaster a civil claim for negligence may arise. This is a claim that an owner may have to meet on his own for standard insurance policies stipulate that it is a condition precedent to recovery that while the trailer is detached it will be securely braked and scotched.

Secure loads

'You must', says the *Highway Code*, 'ensure that any loads carried or towed are secure'. Regulation 97 of MV (C&U) Regulations deals with the maintenance and use of a vehicle so as not to be a danger or nuisance. Stringent obligations are imposed:

(1) Every vehicle and trailer drawn thereby shall at all times be in good condition and the weight distribution, packing, adjustment of passengers and of the load shall at all times be such that no danger is caused, or is likely to be caused, to any person in, or on, the vehicle, or trailer or on a road.

(2) The load carried shall at all times be secured, if necessary by physical restraint other than its own weight, and be in such a position that neither danger nor nuisance is likely to be caused to any person or property by falling or being blown off, or by reason of any other movement of the load.

(3) No vehicle or trailer shall be used for any purpose for which it is so unsuitable as to cause or be likely to cause danger or nuisance. Care should be taken as to the nature and features of the route to be taken for an offence is committed if at any point of the trip it becomes unsuitable. Windsurfers should keep an eye on their boards. It is to be noted that Regulation 97 creates an absolute offence in which a conviction can be recorded irrespective of any good intention on the part of the driver even if there is but a likelihood of danger.

Along with the above should be read Regulation 140 with relation to forward and rearward projections, as also section 76 of RTA 1972 which imposes an obligation to mark and light in certain circumstances. The sailor trailer should be 'prop' conscious and muzzle it with a distinctive canvas bag or bucket, etc. Magistrates tend to take a dim view of unguarded outboards. Masts of course will normally be unstepped, but if

145

not may fall foul of the law or overhead bridges, sometimes with lethal results.

Miscellaneous points

Note: The following states the general position as to small craft trailers but is subject to certain variations, exceptions and amendments. Most of the references are to the Motor Vehicles (Construction and Use) Regulations 1978 (SI 1978 No. 1017 obtainable from HMSO).

Overall length
The overall length of a two-wheeler and load (excluding draw-bar) must not generally exceed 7m (22ft 11in). If four wheels, the maximum length is 12m (Regulation 73).

Overall width
The overall width of the trailer shall not exceed 2.3m (7ft 6in). Subject to certain provisions it may be 2.5m maximum (Regulation 74). The load must not be greater than 2.9m.

Total weight
In general the total laden weight of a trailer together with drawing car must not exceed 24 390 kilogrammes (Regulation 87).

Invalid carriage
An invalid carriage may not draw a trailer (Regulation 132).

Motor cycles
No trailer may be drawn by a motor cycle with not more than two wheels and without a side-car (Regulation 130).

Springs
Trailers must be equipped with suitable and sufficient springs (Regulation 12).

Mirrors
Efficient mirrors (normally three) should be fitted (Regulations 23 and 24).

Wings

Wheels should be fitted with wings, etc. to catch mud or water thrown up by their rotation unless protection is afforded by the body of the vehicle (Regulation 79).

Brakes

In general as from 1st October 1986, trailers must have an efficient braking system. The gross loaded weight must be marked on the trailer (Regulation 75).

Tyres

The trailer must be fitted with pneumatic tyres, or a tyre of soft or elastic material (Regulation 77), not mixed (Regulation 108), in good condition (Regulation 107), and at correct pressure. Spare is advisable.

Lights

By the Road Vehicles Lighting Regulations 1971, all lights must be in an efficient condition. These include: two approved rear red lights; and, since 1st April 1980, connecting stop lights and fog light(s). The number plate must be illuminated. Two red triangular rear reflectors should be displayed. Most trailers should have amber direction indicators. A reversing light is not mandatory. In cases of submersible trailers a special check should be made as to corrosion. Where a load projects more than 1 metre behind a trailer an additional red light must be shown. Detached trailers on the road after dark must show both front and rear lights.

Marking

An approved trailer plate with registration mark of the drawing car must be carried in a conspicuous position on the back (Regulation 81). This must be illuminated during the prescribed hours. The kerbside weight of the car and the gross weight of the trailer should be marked respectively thereon (Regulation 96). The 50 mph limit sign (if applicable) must be displayed. When towing abroad the letters GB must be displayed on the rear of both vehicles in a vertical position.

Speed limits

A motor vehicle drawing one trailer, if a car adapted to carrying not more than 8 passengers, is limited to 40 mph. However a private car drawing one trailer is limited to 50 mph on all open roads (save in a restricted area where a lower limit applies) provided that the conditions in section 8 Road Traffic Regulations 1967 are satisfied. These are: the kerbside weight is marked in or outside the car; trailer is marked with maximum gross weight; rear plate with number 50 on black in white, silver or grey figures is displayed. If the trailer has brakes, laden weight shall not exceed the kerbside weight of the drawing vehicle. If unbraked its laden weight shall not exceed 60% of the kerbside weight of the drawing vehicle.

Roadside checks

A police officer may stop any vehicle on a road for the purposes of a test by an examiner as to the roadworthy condition of the drawing car and trailer. Vehicle offences under the Construction and Use Regulations where danger arises can lead to endorsement of licence, imposition of 3 penalty points and a fine.

Trailing in France

The maximum dimensions for vehicles and trailers on the roads in France are:

Height	no restrictions
Overall width	2.50 m
Overall length	
Motor vehicles (excluded poles) and cable winding devices	11.00 m
Trailers (excluding tow bar)	11.00 m
Articulated vehicles	15.00 m
Vehicles-trailer combination	18.00 m

To import temporarily a vehicle exeeding the permitted dimensions, application should be made for special authorisation to the Préfet at the point of entry.

Belgium

A *carnet de passages en Douane* is required in Belgium for all pleasure craft temporarily imported by road, except craft without motors not exceeding 5.5 metres (18 feet) LOA, and for trailers not accompanied by the towing vehicle. The *carnet* allows a visitor temporarily to import vehicles, boats and outboards for recreational purposes without depositing duty with the local customs authorities. A *carnet* is also required for certain types of craft and engines in other countries such as Finland, Monaco, Luxembourg and Romania. On returning home the onus is on an owner to show that UK VAT has been paid on his boat or equipment, otherwise he may be liable to pay such levy again. Accordingly, those taking boats, boards and outboards, etc. abroad should have with them the supporting registration documents or receipts.

In general

The above is but a brief trailer, so to speak, of the lie of the land on the topic. Like the Goodwin Sands it is a constantly shifting area to chart. A weather eye must be kept on all changes. This is especially so for the DIY enthusiast. If in doubt the RYA, a motoring association, manufacturer, or the police should be consulted. Cardinal Richelieu once said: 'Show me six lines written by the most honest man and I will find something in them to hang him'. A traffic patrol may have similar confidence when looking at the lines of a boat on wheels. The Road Traffic Acts are said to make criminals of all, as well over two million drivers find out in the magistrates' courts in each year. There is a lot to be said for staying out at sea!

Useful Addresses

ADMIRALTY CHART AGENTS
A full list of these is available from the Hydrographic
Department. The leading London agent is:
J. D. Potter Ltd,
145 Minories,
London EC3 NIN
(01) 709 9076

ADVERTISING STANDARDS AUTHORITY
Brook House,
Torrington Place,
London WC1E 7HN
(01)5805555

ARBITRATORS, CHARTERED INSTITUTE OF
75 Cannon Street,
London EC4 N5BH
(01)2368761

ASSOCIATION OF BRITISH INSURERS
Aldermary House,
Queen Street,
London EC4N 1TT
(01) 248 4477

ASSOCIATION OF BRITISH SAILMAKERS
as at Boating Industry House

ASSOCIATION OF BROKERS & YACHT AGENTS
as at Boating Industry House

BOAT WORLD
Haymarket Publishing Ltd,
38–42 Hampton Road,
Teddington,
Middlesex TW11 0JE
(01) 977 8787
(This is the boating trade yearbook and directory for all useful
addresses relating to sail and powercraft.)

BOATING INDUSTRY HOUSE
Vale Road,
Oatlands Park,
Weybridge,
Surrey KT13 9NS
(0932) 54511

BRITISH BOATING INDUSTRY
as at Boating Industry House (above)

BRITISH CONSUL
Telegraphic address: 'BRITAIN', followed by name of town.

BRITISH HIRE CRUISER FEDERATION
as at Boating Industry House (above)

BRITISH STANDARDS INSTITUTION
2 Park Street,
London W1
(01) 629 9000

BRITISH SUB-AQUA CLUB
16 Upper Woburn Place,
London WC1 H0QW
(01) 387 9302

BRITISH TELECOM INTERNATIONAL
Maritime and Aeronautical Radio,
43 Bartholomew Close,
London EC1A 7HP
(01) 583 9416

BRITISH WATERWAYS BOARD
Melbury House,
Melbury Terrace,
London NW1 6JX
(01) 262 6711

CRUISING ASSOCIATION
Ivory House,
St Katherine's Dock,
World Trade Centre,
London E1 9AT
(01) 481 0881

CHARTS
(see Admiralty Chart Agents)

DEBRETT'S REGISTER OF YACHTS
Debrett's Peerage Ltd,
73/77 Britannia Road,
London SW6 2JR
(01) 736 6524/5/6

DEPARTMENT OF THE ENVIRONMENT
43 Marsham Street,
London SW1 P3PY
(01) 212 3434

FAIR TRADING, OFFICE OF
Field House,
15–25 Breams' Buildings,
London EC4A 1PR
(01) 242 2858

FRENCH GOVERNMENT TOURIST OFFICE
178 Piccadilly,
London W1V 0AL
(01) 499 6911

HAMMICK'S BOOKSHOPS LTD
Sweet & Maxwell,

116 Chancery Lane,
London WC2A 1PP
(For all legal books and journals, etc.)
(01)405 5711

HM COASTGUARD
as for Department of Trade (below)

HM CUSTOMS and EXCISE
Dorset House,
Stamford Street,
London SE1 9PS
(01) 928 0533

HM STATIONERY OFFICE
49 High Holborn,
London WC1V 6HB
(01) 211 5656
(Callers only)
PO Box 276
London SW8 5DT
(Trade and London area mail orders)

HYDROGRAPHIC DEPARTMENT
Ministry of Defence,
Taunton,
Somerset TA1 2DN
(0823) 87900

INLAND WATERWAYS ASSOCIATION
114 Regents Park Road,
London NW1 8UQ
(01) 586 2556

INSURANCE OMBUDSMAN BUREAU
31 Southampton Row,
London WC1B 5HJ
(01)242 8613

IRISH TOURIST BOARD
Ireland House,
150 New Bond Street,

London W1
(01) 629 7292

INTERNATIONAL YACHT RACING UNION
60 Knightsbridge,
London SW1X 7JX
(01) 253 6221

LAW SOCIETY
The Law Society's Hall,
113 Chancery Lane,
London WC2A 1PL
(01) 242 1222

LLOYD'S LAW REPORTS
Sheepen Place,
Colchester CO3 3LP
(0206) 69222

LLOYD'S REGISTER OF SHIPPING
71 Fenchurch Street,
London EC3M 4BS
(01) 709 9166

LLOYD'S REGISTER OF SHIPPING
(YACHT and SMALL CRAFT DEPARTMENT)
69 Oxford Street,
Southampton SO1 1DL
(0703) 220353

MACMILLAN & SILK CUT NAUTICAL ALMANAC
Dept AH, Macmillan
4 Little Essex Street,
London WC2R 3LF
(01) 836 6633

MARINE TRADES ASSOCIATION
as at Boating Industry House

METROPOLITAN POLICE
Thames Division,
98 Wapping High Street,
London E1 9NE
(01) 488 5212

NATIONAL BOAT SHOWS LTD
as at Boating Industry House

NATIONAL FEDERATION OF SAILING SCHOOLS
as at Boating Industry House

NATIONAL YACHT HARBOUR ASSOCIATION
as at Boating Industry House

PORT OF LONDON AUTHORITY
Thames House,
St Andrews Road,
Tilbury,
Essex
(03752) 3444

POTTER, J. D. LTD
see Admiralty Chart Agents

RADIO REGULATORY DIVISION
Department of Trade and Industry,
Waterloo Bridge House,
Waterloo Road,
London SE1 8UA
(01) 275 3316

ROYAL CRUISING CLUB
42 Half Moon Street,
London W1
(01) 499 2103

REED'S NAUTICAL ALMANAC
Thomas Reed Publications Ltd,

36/7 Cock Lane,
London EC1A 9BY
(01) 248 7881

REGISTER GENERAL OF SHIPPING & SEAMEN
Department of Trade,
Llantrisant Road,
Cardiff CF5 2YS
(0222) 561 221

REGISTRAR OF BRITISH SHIPS
Custom House,
Lower Thames Street,
London EC3
(01) 626 1515

ROYAL NATIONAL LIFEBOAT INSTITUTION
West Quay Road,
Poole,
Dorset BH15 1HZ
(0202) 671133

ROYAL OCEAN RACING CLUB
20 St James's Place,
London SW1A 1NN
(01) 493 5252

ROYAL SOCIETY FOR THE PREVENTION OF ACCIDENTS
Cannon House,
The Priory,
Queensway,
Birmingham B4 6BS
(021) 233 2461

ROYAL YACHTING ASSOCIATION
Victoria Way,
Woking,
Surrey GU21 1EQ
(048 62) 5022

SHIP & BOAT BUILDERS NATIONAL FEDERATION
as at Boating Industry House

SOLENT CRUISING and RACING ASSOCIATION
18/19 Bath Road,
Cowes,
Isle of Wight PO31 7QN
(0983) 295744

THAMES WATER AUTHORITY
Thames Conservancy Division,
Nugent House,
Vastern Road,
Reading,
Berks RG1 8DB
(0734) 593275

TRINITY HOUSE (Corporation of)
Trinity House,
Tower Hill,
London EC3N 4DH
(01) 480 6601

**YACHT BROKERS, DESIGNERS & SURVEYORS
ASSOCIATION**
Orchard Hill,
The Avenue,
Haselmere,
Surrey
(Haselmere) 4329

YACHT CHARTER ASSOCIATION
60 Silverdale,
New Milton,
Hants BH25 7DE
(New Milton) 619004

Index

AA, 142
Abersoch, 50, 127
ABYA, 13, 21
acceptance, 13–15
addresses, useful, 150–57
admiralty actions, 119
advertisements, 13, 14, 138, 150
agent, 20, 150
agony of the moment, 91
aground, 89
aliens, 38, 98, 99, 136, 139
almanacs, 1, 11, 154–5
anchoring, 68, 84, 85, 88–9, 111,
    113, 123, 128, 131
animals, 95, 97, 101–102
Annie Hay, 110
apportionment, 82, 87, 112
APR, 31
arbitration, 17, 33, 37, 62, 74, 91,
    120, 150
arrest, 71, 105, 108, 119, 133
arrivals, 96
as she lies, 22, 25
assault, 121, 127
assessors, 78
assist, duty to, 139
assured, 47
Atomic Energy Act 1954, 127
auctions, 14, 25, 33

Bab Ballads, 64
bank
    loan, 13, 28, 31
    reference, 19, 36

bankruptcy of builder, 18
    (*see also* insolvency)
banned areas, 128
Bantry Bay, 115
bareboat charter, 34, 36
bathing, 126, 127
Belloc H, 66
berthing, 113–14
Bill of Sale, 13, 23, 24
birds, 97
Birkenhead, 139
births, 134
Bische, 7
blight, 134–5
boat, 7
    shows, 155
    world, 151
bonded stores, 38, 99
book list, 11
bottled gas, 59, 114
bottomry, 71
Bradshaw v. *Ewart James*, 81
Bramley Moore, 53
breach of contract, 17
Brest/Elbe, 55
British
    Boating Industry, 21, 151
    Consul, 24, 38, 41, 94, 97, 151
    Standards, 59, 60, 151
    Telecom, 136, 151
    Waterways Act, 9, 152
brochures, 15
brokers, 19, 20, 22, 150
Brownsea, 126, 130
BSAC, 114, 131, 151

builder's certificate, 41
buoys, 76, 111, 125, 128
burden of proof, 43, 68, 70, 72, 90,
    97, 102, 104, 119, 128, 149
burgee, 46
burials, 134
buying
    new, 15–17
    secondhand, 19
bye-laws, 3, 65, 76, 93, 123, 124,
    126, 138
Bynershoek, 9
Bywell Castle, 91

CA, 152
cables, 124, 128
cannon shot rule, 9
Cardigan, Lord, 111
careless sailing, 90, 91, 126
Cargo Bonito, 72
Carlsen, K, 2
Carroll, L, 13, 47, 65, 94
carving, 42
cats, 95, 97, 101–102
Caudebec, 55
caveat emptor, 22, 50
CB radio, 138
certificate
    British Registry, 42, 94
    firearms, 135
Channel Islands, 3, 49, 94, 106
Channel, narrow, 84, 117
Charles II, 6
charter, 32, 33–7, 45, 51, 56, 94, 107
charterparty, 34, 36–7
charts, 2, 9, 68, 84, 92, 117, 150
cheques, 23, 97
Chesterton, G K, 77
Childers, E, 2
Churchill, Sir W, 73
Citizens Band radio, 138
civil
    proceedings, 119–20
    time limits, 118
clearance, 99
clubs, 5, 39, 45, 46, 106, 135
coastal waters, 55
Coastguard, HM, 75, 94, 153

Coleridge, Lord, 139
collision regulations, 6, 7, 11, 68,
    78–93
collisions
    recording, 91–3
    reporting, 92–3
colours, 95
commission, agents', 19, 20, 21
Commissioner of Oaths, 24, 41
common law, 3, 32
compensation, 130, 131
complaints, insurance, 63
conditions and warranties, 16, 28
Conrad, J, 2
conservation areas, 123
constructive total loss, 52
Consul, British, 24, 38
Consumer Credit Act 1974, 29, 30
consumer protection, 11, 20, 63
Continental Shelf Act 1964, 10, 128
contracts, 13, 118
contributory negligence, 112–13
courts
    Coroners, 57
    County, 119, 127, 130
    Crown, 4, 121, 136, 138
    High, 62, 81, 119
    Magistrates', 81, 86, 121, 123,
        127, 149
Cowes, 3
craft, 7
credit sale, 30
crew, 60, 69, 116, 133, 139
crime, 82, 86
    prevention, 131–3
criminal damage, 127, 130
Crowhurst, D, 2
Crown Court, 4, 121, 130
Crown Proceedings Act 1947, 72
Curacoa HMS, 78
custom built boat, 16
customs, HM, 24, 40, 42, 96–106,
    153
Customs and Excise Management
    Act 1979, 7, 55, 104–105
customs duty, 94

damage, criminal, 127, 130

damages, 18
Darling, Lord, 93
deaths, 98, 134
Debrett's Register of Yachts, 39, 152
declaration of ownership, 41
Defects Liability Clause, 17
Defence, Ministry of, 5, 44, 127, 128
definitions, 6–10
delivery of yachts, 16, 25, 36, 64
demurrage, 25
Denning, Lord, 27, 53, 117
departures, 96
deposits, 15, 35
derelict, 10
dinghy, 50, 61, 68, 111, 122, 132, 144
direction finders, 50
Director of Public Prosecutions, 124
discipline, 108
dishonest handling, 132
Disraeli, B, 90
distress signals, 72, 95, 135, 137, 138
Distress Signals Order 1977, 78
divers, 4, 111, 114, 115, 131
Divina SS, 87
dock master, 9
documents, overseas, 94–5
dogs, 95, 97, 101–102
Dover Straits, 87
drugs, 99–100, 101, 121
Dulcibella, 2
Dumping at Sea Act, 134
Dunraven, Lord, 109
duty, 97
duty free, 98, 99, 102

EEC, 5, 95, 104, 136, 142
Eire, 94, 102, 107, 142, 153
Elizabeth I, 125
Emerson, 69
Enchantress, 111
Ensign
   blue, 44
   red, 44, 95
   privileged, 5, 9, 38, 95, 106
   special, 44–6
   white, 44, 103
EPIRB, 138
equity, 4, 32
European Communities Act 1972, 104
evidence, 91, 92, 120, 132–3
Exchange and Mart, 13

Fair Trading, Office of, 20, 63, 152
Falmouth, 110
false signals, 125, 138
Fastnet disaster, 73
finance, 13, 28–31
fire, 68, 114
fire extinguisher, 59
firearms, 135–6
firing ranges, 128
Fishery Limits Act, 10, 136
fishing vessels, 7, 37, 43, 85, 89
flags, 4, 38, 44–6, 95, 97
flares, 60, 69, 135
flick knives, 101
flotsam, 10
fog, 80
Forbes, Sir Hugh, 73, 141
force majeur, 16
foreign, going, 94, 122
foreshore, 126–7
forfeiture, 103–105
Fortunity, 37
Four of Hearts, 37
France, 94, 97, 106–107, 122, 148, 152
Frances, 113
free pratique, 99, 103
fuel, 59
full report, 98

Gas, bottled, 35, 59, 114
gas lines, 128
gash, 114
Geneva Convention, 10, 128
Gilbert, W S, 64, 139
giving way, 83
Gladstone, W, 90
glues, 112
Gray, Thomas, 78

guarantees, 31
guarantors, 31
Guide to Government Publications, 2
guns, 135–6

Hale, Lord, 124
Harbour Master, 4, 9, 46, 70, 75–6, 122, 133
harbours, 9, 117
harness, safety, 60, 68
head on, 83
Herbert A P, 3, 143
Highland Lock, 113
Highway Code, 143
hire–purchase, 19, 30–31
HMSO, 2, 12, 153
Holyhead, 50
Home Office, 100, 115, 130
home trade limits, 99
houseboats, 8, 26, 56
hovercraft, 3, 7
Hydrographer of the Royal Navy, 9, 84, 150, 153

Ialine, 89
Ilfracombe, 124
illegality, 62, 105
immigration, 98, 99
importation, 101
in commission, 49, 55
Inland Revenue, 43
inland waters, 55, 153
insolvency of
    advertiser, 14
    builder, 18, 64
instalment contracts, 18, 30
Institute Yacht Clauses, 49
insurance, 47–64, 150
    all risks extension, 52
    arbitration, 62
    bank loan, 31
    Brest/Elbe, 55
    cancellation, 63
    Channel Islands, 106
    complaints, 63
    craning, 64
    cruising range, 54–5

death, 31
deliveries, 25
dinghies, 50, 61–2
duty of disclosure, 50
fire, 19, 59
flares, 60
gas, 59
houseboats, 8, 26, 56, 111
household policy, 52
illegality, 62, 105
illness, 31, 57
in commission, 49, 55
inland waters, 55
insolvency, 19, 64
Institute of Yacht Clauses, 49
insurable interest, 48
jury service, 36
laid up, 49, 55
legal charges, 57
life jackets, 59
limitation of liability, 53–4
Lloyds', 47
loss/damage, 56
Marine Insurance Act 1906, 47, 50
marine mortgage, 28
medical, 57
no claims, 57
non–transferable, 63
notification, 57
Ombudsman, 49, 153
outboards, 50
overseas, 95
partial loss, 52–3
partnership, 33
personal effects, 50, 61
policy, 54–63
premium, 50, 65
proposal form, 49–50
questionnaire, 51
racing extension clause, 61
renewal date, 63
repairs, 56
reporting, 56, 57
safety harness, 59–60
safety requirements, 58–9
salvage charges, 61
seaworthiness, 58–9
standard yacht policy, 54–63

161

surveyors, 26
tenders, 60
theft, 19
third party risks, 54
total loss, 52
tow, 56, 61
trailers, 50
transfer, 63
uberrimae fidei, 50
unemployment, 31
use, 56
valuation, 51–2
windsurfers, 62
intended depature, notice, 96–7
interest, 29
International Code of Signals, 2
International Monetary Fund, 54
International Regulations for
    Prevention of Collisions at
    Sea, 6, 7, 68, 78–93
Interpretation Act, 1
inventory, 23, 32, 36
Ireland
    Northern, 3, 102, 142
    Republic of, 94, 102, 107, 142,
    153
Isle of Man, 3, 55, 102
IYRU, 5, 110–11, 154

jetsam, 10
Johnson, Dr, 6
joy riding, 129–30
jurisdiction, 4, 9, 97, 121
jury
    service, 36
    trial by, 81, 121, 125
Justices of the Peace, 24, 41, 81,
    86, 121, 145

Kenyon, Lord, 3
Kipling, R, 109, 141
Kirk, K, 136
Knaresboro, 84

lagan, 10
laid up, 49, 55
Lane, Lord, 100
launch, 8, 115

Law Reform (Contributory
    Negligence) Act, 112
law reports, 3
Law Society, 116, 154
legal charges, 57, 62
library, ship's, 1–2, 97
licences
    CB, 138
    radio, 136–8
    TV, 137
liens, 19, 70–71, 77
lifeboat, 72
    (*see also* RNLI)
lifebuoy, 68, 132
lifejacket, 59, 68, 107
liferaft, 68, 132
light dues, 76
lighthouses, 76, 128
lights, 68, 87–8
limitation of liability, 53–4, 109–110
liquidation, *see* insolvency
Lloyds', 47
    Series Production Certificate, 16
    Law Reports, 3, 154
    Yacht Services, 17, 154
loan, 30, 31
lobster pots, 131
log, 92, 133
London, 82–3
    Convention, 53
    Port of, 3, 81, 89
look out, 82, 91
Loss
    constructive, 52
    total, 52
Lyon v. *Oxford*, 141

Magistrates' courts, 81, 86, 99
Malicious Damage Act 1861, 125
Malta GC, 69
Mansfield, Lord, 120
manslaughter, 124
marina, 33, 47, 61, 67, 130, 137, 143
    sales, 20
Marine Insurance Act 1906, 47, 50
Mariner's Handbook, 2
Maritime Conventions Act 1911,
    75, 82, 112, 118, 139

marking vessels, 38, 42, 43
marking wrecks, 76
mast, 27, 61, 88, 145
Mayday, 72, 138
medical charges, 57, 95
mens rea, 82
Merchant Shipping
   Acts 1894–1983, 3, 6, 37, 43, 44,
     53, 67–8, 74, 80–81, 110, 124
   (Carriage of Nautical
     Publication) Rules 1975, 2
   (Distress Signals and Prevention
     of Collision) Regulations 1983,
     78–93
   (Fees) Regulations, 30
   (Fire Appliance) Rules, 68
   (Liability of Shipowners and
     Others) Act 1958, 53
   (Life Saving Appliances) Rules, 68
   Notices, 2
   (Safety Convention) Act 1949,
     138
mid–channel, 84
Mignonette, 139
minors, 31, 37, 62, 83
misrepresentation, 14, 19, 40, 43, 51
Misuse of Drugs Act 1971, 99–100
MOD warrant, 44
Moorcock, 113
moorings, 9, 22, 46, 47, 50, 65–7, 123
mortgage, 13, 22, 23, 26, 28–30, 38,
   42, 43, 47
Motor Vehicle (Construction and
   Use) Regulations, 58, 142–8
murder, 121, 139
mutiny, 108, 133

name, 1, 39–41, 43, 132
narrow channels, 84, 89
national parks, 123
nautical assessors, 78
navigation
   art, 128
   rights, 128, 123, 126, 134
Navy List, 45
negligence, 26, 27, 28, 54, 59, 66,
   69, 80, 82, 87, 90, 91, 111–120,
   144

no claims discount, 57
no cure: no pay, 74
noise, 133
Nona, 66
non-patrial, 99
Norfolk Broads, 34, 37
Normand, Lord, 118
Northern Ireland, 3, 102, 142
notice of intended departure, 96–7
notice to mariners, 2
Nuclear Installation Act 1965, 127
nuisance, 133–4
NYHA, 67, 155

oars, 7, 88
obstruction, 76, 134
offer and acceptance, 13–15
Official Secrets Act, 127
oil, 134
   rigs, 4, 10, 128–9
Ombudsman, 5, 49
outboards, 60, 132
overtaking, 83
oyster beds, 128, 131

Padstow, 121
Pagham Nature Reserve, 123
paints
   anti-foul, 131
   dangerous, 112
particulars of craft, 15, 22
partnership, 4, 13, 31–3
passenger certificate, 7
passports, 94, 97, 98, 108
patrials, 43, 134, 136
penalty clauses, 17, 35
Pepler, H P D, 1
Pepys, Samuel, 5
personal effects, 50, 61
personal injuries, 118
pets, 95, 97, 101–102
Phelan, Judge, 11, 74
pilotage, 6, 76
piracy, 48, 121
planning controls, 135
pleasure boat, 7–8, 38, 43, 96
Pleasure Craft (Arrival and
   Report) Regulations, 7, 96–9

Plimsoll line, 42
police, 94, 103, 132, 133, 135, 142,
    148, 149, 155
pollution, 10, 90, 134
Poole, 65, 130
Port Health Authority, 103
Port of London Act 1969, 81
Port of London Authority, 3, 89,
    155
pratique, 99, 103
Prevention of Pollution Act, 134
Princess Alice, 91
printed terms, 77
private sales, 20, 21, 23
production boat, 15, 25
professional negligence, 27
Protection of Wrecks Act, 128
Public Health Acts, 103, 125–6
Public Health (Ships) Regulation
    Act, 1970, 99, 102–103

Q flag, 95, 97, 98, 99, 106
quantum meruit, 74–5, 77
quarantine, 102
Queen Mary, 78
quick report procedure, 98

rabies, 95, 101–102, 106
RAC, 142
racing, 56, 61, 109–11
radar, 50
    reflector, 60, 69
    scanner, 87
radio, 5, 9, 50, 136–8, 155
RAF, 72, 116
rape, 121
rates, 9, 121
RCC, 155
reading list, 11
receiver of wreck, 10
recording collisions, 91–3
red ensigns, 44, 95
refrigerators, 114
Regatta, 109, 122
register of ships, 37–43
Registrar General of Shipping and
    Seamen, 39, 156
registration, 37–43, 106

repairs, 77, 98, 101
reporting
    arrival, 98
    collisions, 92–3
    crimes, 133
rescue, 72–5
retention clause, 16
Rhodian code, 4
Richelieu, Cardinal, 149
RNLI, 72–3, 156
road, 142–3
Road Traffic Acts, 142
rockets, 135
RORC, 69, 73, 156
ROSPA, 156
Royal Navy, 72
rudder, 112
Rules of Supreme Court, 91–3, 119
Rumpheimer v. *Haddock*, 143
RYA, 5, 43, 73, 74, 97, 110, 137,
    142, 156
RYS, 44, 111

safety rules, 58, 67–9
sailing and steering rules, 82–8
Saint Paul, 69
sale, private, 20, 21, 23
Sale of Goods Act, 13, 16
salvage, 10, 52, 61, 62, 69–71, 73, 74
Satanita, 109
SBBNF, 16, 19, 21, 114, 157
Scilly Isles, 125
Scotland, 3
Sea Fisheries Acts, 131
sea lawyer, 3
sea marks, 125
seaman, 121
search, 103
Seaway Code, 2, 83, 111
seaworthy, 58–9, 69
secondhand boat, 19, 25
security deposit, 35
Seine, R, 55
separation schemes, 78, 81, 84–7
service of writs, 119
Shakespeare, W, 121
shares in ships, 32, 38
sharing boat, 31–33

ship
  defined, 6
  library, 1
  name, 1
  papers, 94
  unseaworthy, 67-8, 124
ship to shore, licence, 136-7
signals
  distress, 50, 69, 72, 135, 138
  false, 125
  sound, 68, 92
silencer, 126
Silver Mist, 130
skiers, 56, 107, 112, 124
Skye, 125
Slocum, J, 2
small craft, 96
Small Ships' Register, 5, 6, 43-4,
  95, 107
smuggling, 62, 100, 101-106, 121,
  125
Snark, 76
sole agent, 20
sole selling agent, 20
solent, 157
solicitors, 3, 11, 24, 87, 116-17, 120
sonic booms, 56
sound signals, 88
speed, 82-3, 89, 91, 107, 114, 126
Spray, 2
stage payments, 16
standard terms, 15, 19, 77
statutes, 3, 80
steering rules, 78-93
stores, 99
Sub Aqua Club, 114, 131
subject to
  all faults, 22
  contract, 15
  mortgage, 15
  survey, 15, 21
submarine cables, 124, 128
Submarine Telegraph Act 1885, 124
suicide, 62
Sullivan, Sergeant, 115
Supply of Goods (Implied Terms)
    Act 1973, 16
Supreme Court (*see* rules of)

survey
  engine, 26
  report, 22, 26, 29
surveyors, 22, 25-7, 41-2
syndicate, 32-3

taking a boat without authority,
    122, 129-30
Taku, 103-104
Teddington Lock, 40, 89, 135
television, 137
tenders, 60
territorial waters, 9, 136
Thames, 3, 69, 76, 89-91
Thames Conservancy Acts, 90
Thames Water Authority, 8, 40,
  90, 157
Thanet, Isle of, 126
theft, 127, 131, 138
Theft Act 1968, 129, 132
third party liability, 54
tidal waters, 9, 123
time limits, 118
title, 23, 31, 38, 41, 43
tools, 112
Torquay, 66
tort, 3, 119
total loss, 52-3
tow, 56, 61, 70-72, 75, 90
Towerfield SS, 117
Town and Country Planning Acts,
  135
Trade, Department of, 5, 57, 68,
  85, 87, 92, 136
Trade Descriptions Act, 14
traffic separation scheme, 78, 81,
  84-7
trailers, 141-9
  AA, 142
  Belgium, 149
  brakes, 147
  carnet, 149
  detached, 144
  examiners, 148
  French regulations, 107, 148
  Highway Code, 143, 145
  immobilising, 144
  insurance, 58, 143, 144

invalid carriage, 146
learners, 144
length, 146
lights, 147
load, 145
Lyon v. *Oxford*, 141
marking, 147
masts, 145
measurements, 146
mirrors, 146
MOT certificate, 144
motor cycle, 146
outboards, 145
passengers, 144
penalties, 144, 148
projections, 145, 147
regulations, 58, 142
secure load, 145
speed, 148
springs, 146
tyres, 147
weight, 146
width, 146
wings, 147
Transport, Department of, 5, 43
transporation, 64
trawling nets, 128
trespass, 66, 126–8
Trinity House, 5, 80, 157
Troutbeck, Reverend, 125
Truculent, HMS, 87
TV licence, 131

uberrimae fidei, 50
UK coastal and inland, 55
Unfair Contract Terms Act, 27–8
unseaworthy, 67–8, 124
USA, 122

vaccination, 107
Valkyrie, 109

valuation, 15, 33, 49, 51–2
vampire, 102
vandalism, 50, 65, 130, 131
VAT, 16, 21, 23, 30, 95, 97, 98, 99,
    101, 149
Verey pistols, 135
vessel, 6, 79
VHF, 5
visa, 94
Viscount, 72–3
volenti non fit injuria, 115

warrant, royal, 44
warranties, 16, 28
wash, 90, 114
water police, 103
waterguard, 103
waters, 9, 55
Waterways Board, 9, 12
Weller, Sam, 92
wills, 116
winding up (*see* insolvency)
windsurfers, 4, 62, 132, 145
Winters, J, 142
Wireless Telegraphy Acts, 136
witnesses, 91
wrecks, 10, 76, 128
write, service of, 119

Yacht Boat Safety Scheme, 75, 94,
    97
Yacht Charter Association, 34–5
Yacht, defined, 6
Yacht Insurance clauses, 49
Yachting Monthly, 35
YBDSA, 13, 21, 26, 27, 157
YCA, 34, 157
YG, 87

zones, traffic, 85